After graduating and teaching at S[...] in 1987, Mi[ck ...] complete [...] Education d[egree ...] University of Western Australia. His affinity for words and a premature mid-life crisis then saw him study journalism at Curtin University and he has contributed to a number of sports and health magazines, including *Australian Rugby News* and *Inside Sport*. He moved from journalism to advertising, where his writing has been awarded at the international level. Also a modern-day poet, he has recited his work on radio and television and had it published in national newspapers and magazines. He was awarded 'Best Sports Poem in 2002' by *Sydney Morning Herald* columnist and bestselling author Peter FitzSimons.

Mick also enjoys sports commentary and has called international water polo tournaments on TV and the National League finals on local radio. He is the chief rugby commentator on Radio 6PR and was the code's only finalist in the Best Sports Coverage category of the 2007 Australian Commercial Radio Awards.

Mick is married with two young boys and by day is a Director of Cooch Creative, a regional advertising and marketing consultancy. He lives in Mt Hawthorn, Perth, next door to Alistair Box, a former team mate at UWA who always showered after games with his Speedos on.

HOW FOUR RUGBY MATES REALISED THEIR DREAM OF PLAYING FOR AUSTRALIA

Mick Colliss

ABC Books

 The ABC 'Wave' device is a trademark of the Australian Broadcasting Corporation and is used under licence by HarperCollins*Publishers* Australia.

First published in Australia in 2009
by HarperCollins*Publishers* Australia Pty Limited
ABN 36 009 913 517
www.harpercollins.com.au

Copyright © Mick Colliss 2009

The right of Mick Colliss to be identified as the author of this work has been asserted by him in accordance with the *Copyright Amendment (Moral Rights) Act 2000.*

This work is copyright. Apart from any use as permitted under the *Copyright Act 1968*, no part may be reproduced, copied, scanned, stored in a retrieval system, recorded, or transmitted, in any form or by any means, without the prior written permission of the publisher.

HarperCollins*Publishers*
25 Ryde Road, Pymble, Sydney, NSW 2073, Australia
31 View Road, Glenfield, Auckland 0627, New Zealand
A 53, Sector 57, Noida, UP, India
77–85 Fulham Palace Road, London W6 8JB, United Kingdom
2 Bloor Street East, 20th floor, Toronto, Ontario M4W 1A8, Canada
10 East 53rd Street, New York NY 10022, USA

National Library of Australia Cataloguing-in-Publication data:

Colliss, Mick.
    Full-contact Sudoku: how four rugby mates realised their
    dream of playing for Australia / Mick Colliss.
    ISBN: 978 0 7333 2644 8 (pbk)
    Colliss, Mick. Sudoku — Australia.
    Mathematical recreations — Australia.
793.74092

Cover and internal design by Jane Waterhouse
Cover images: pencil and rugby ball by Shutterstock.com,
    all other images courtesy of the author
Author photograph © Craig Kinder, F22
Sudoku puzzles © WSC3/Quixy. Created by Deb Mohanty
Picture-section design by Ingrid Kwong
Typeset in 11/15.5pt Baskerville BE Regular by Kirby Jones
Printed and bound in Australia by Griffin Press
70gsm Classic used by HarperCollins*Publishers* is a natural, recyclable product made from wood grown in sustainable forests. The manufacturing processes conform to the environmental regulations in the country of origin, Finland.

7 6 5 4 3 2   09 10 11 12

To anyone who's ever dreamed of
wearing the green and gold

Contents

	Foreword	xi
1	Planting the seed	1
2	Lawn bowls	11
3	What's sudoku?	18
4	Never say never	22
5	*Star Trek* and comic books	32
6	It's a boy	37
7	Conditions apply	44
8	Pressure	53
9	Regrets	59
10	I'm in	67
11	Opportunities	70
12	Picked	74
13	Mates	81
14	Lights, camera, action	86
15	Rocky Balboa	92
16	Damn you, Andrew Symonds	99
17	The breakthrough	108
18	Damn you, Andrew Symonds (Part II)	111
19	Dog's balls	117
20	Mark Skiffington, Captain of Australia	127
21	Playing for Australia	135
22	World ranking	141
23	Come on Australia	151
24	Hard beds, soft stools	158
25	The wrap-up	163
	Honour roll	169
	Backword	171
	Acknowledgements	175

PLAYING FOR AUSTRALIA

When I was young I had a dream
To one day wear the gold and green
A member of our Wallaby team
Playing for Australia.

To walk onto the SCG
Forty thousand cheering me
Heart rate beating, frantically
Playing for Australia.

National anthem, tear-filled eyes
Emotions that I can't disguise
My first test cap a treasured prize
Playing for Australia.

Score the try that wins the game
Team mates shouting out my name
A thrill I simply can't explain
Playing for Australia.

Cold beer in the dressing shed
A million thoughts run through my head
Wouldn't care if I dropped dead.
I'd played for Australia.

To be one of the chosen few
To say, 'I've made my test debut'
There's nothing that I wouldn't do
To represent Australia.

And that's the truth because it seems
I finally made a national team
Chased and caught the elusive dream
Of playing for Australia.

Though it's not rugby, that is true
The game is known as su-do-ku
Not what I'd hoped but it'll do
I've played for Australia.

Foreword

I first came across Mick Colliss when I was sent his book of sporting poetry *What Rhymes with Jakovich?*. Over the years I had become quite fond of sports poetry through a great mate of mine and a fellow Brothers rugby club team mate from Brisbane, Rupert McCall.

Now if someone yells out 'rugby player', poetry is not the immediate association – not Colliss nor McCall style poetry anyway. But nothing surprises me about rugby people. Perhaps because it is a game for, at times, the deepest of specialists. Its people are, at times, quite peculiar. In fact, the greatest thing about rugby is its diversity of characters, and it doesn't matter which team or at which level you play, it's just the same.

Typically there is the serious, accountant-like, mousy-shy industrious player. There is the joker, the closet intellectual, the at times tasteless, at times remorseless, at times sympathetic, and the at all times passionate player … and that's just the tight-head prop. That's the nature of our sport.

Mick Colliss is just one of the characters of our game, a fact that comes through as strongly in this book as it does in the sudokumentary. Mick played rugby for many years with and against some of Australia's greatest internationals, men like Marty Roebuck, Dick Harry and Phil Kearns. He even came in contact with Steve Cutler. I'll let him tell the stories. Although he never pulled on the green and gold of the Wallabies himself, his determination to represent his country didn't die with the selectors' myopia but was ignited with his (self-) selection in the Australian sudoku team for the World Championships in India.

In his book *Full-Contact Sudoku*, the reader can share the highs and the lows of a sporting and sudoku career through Mick's own clever and insightful eyes.

I remember how surprised we were when we discovered that our half-back Rupert was a poet, and one of some ability. Now as we reminisce, we recount fondly how we knew him before he rhymed. Now, I didn't know Mick before he rhymed, but I did know of him before he represented Australia in sudoku.

Here's to a great read and a great Australian sudoku representative!

John Eales

CHAPTER 1

Planting the seed

Martin Luther King isn't the only one who had a dream. Granted, his had global implications and prompted the Civil Rights Act of 1964. Mine was somewhat more insular. Insignificant in comparison. But it was still a dream.

For as long as I can remember, I've wanted to play for Australia. To don the green and gold, and represent my country. It's one of those romantic illusions that has inspired generations of schoolboys to pick up a cricket bat or pull on a pair of boots.

I've lost count of the number of test matches I've had the privilege of watching live. And when I look back at the number of hours I've spent watching them on TV, I'm amazed I'm not some oversized version of a fat kid in a tight shirt and high pants.

The thing is, I never just sat there and watched. Every game, without exception, I imagined myself out there in the middle, trucking it up, making tackles, hitting runs, taking wickets. My heart rate was elevated from the first whistle to the last. I was watching Australia play and dreaming of one day playing for my country.

Life was blissfully simple. And it all made total sense.

Why wouldn't I want to be Dennis Lillee? Walking back to my mark with the crowd chanting my name like it was some religious mantra. Steaming in from the river end, shirt undone to the waist, gold chain bouncing against my broad, bronzed chest. A picture of balance on delivery, the crowd oohing as the new ball flies off the pitch and whistles past the batsman's chin. A follow-through that finishes an inch from my opponent's nose. My forefinger like a wiper blade as it removes a layer of sweat from my brow.

Why wouldn't I want to be David Campese? Mesmerising defences with my trademark goosestep in front of 80,000 spectators. Chipping over the top and regathering. Stepping left, stepping right, stepping left, stepping right. Diving to score a try so amazing even the opposition's fans can't help but stand and applaud.

Why wouldn't I want that?

Playing for Australia seemed the perfect existence. Xanadu. You travelled the world and plied your trade in front of adoring crowds. You made others happy doing what you loved. People you'd never met would come up and pat you on the back and say, 'Well played'.

Wallabies, Kangaroos, the weathered cricketers peering from beneath their treasured baggy greens. There was always something magical about those men. They seemed bigger than average. Stronger than average. Tougher than average. They were real men. Nothing fazed them. They walked tall. They were proud. And I wanted to be just like them.

I wanted to walk out onto the MCG in front of a packed house on Boxing Day and see a banner with 'Mick Colliss for PM' hanging on the fence in front of the Members Stand.

I wanted people to cheer *me* when I opened the batting for Australia and went on to score a double century. I wanted people to cheer *me* when I crossed for the winning try to keep the Bledisloe Cup in Australia. I wanted people to cheer *me* when I stood on the dais to collect my Olympic gold medal.

I never saw the injuries, the failures or the many hours of training. The long trips away from family. All I saw was the glory. It all seemed so attainable. I'd imagined it so many times. It wasn't a matter of if, more a matter of when.

As time passed, so did my idols. Terry Randall turned into Ray Price turned into Wayne Pearce. Dougie Walters turned into John Dyson turned into Mark Taylor. Simon Poidevin turned into David Wilson turned into George Smith. But my dream stayed the same. I wanted to play for Australia.

I remember meeting my first Wallaby like it was yesterday. I was playing junior rugby for Hillview in Eastwood, New South Wales, and we won an Under 15 knockout competition at Manly. Gary Pearse, the former Port Hacking and Randwick flanker, presented me with my pennant on Manly Oval.

When he shook my hand, I felt ten feet tall. *I'd met Gary Pearse, the Wallaby.* It was a defining moment. Like I'd been anointed. Part of me felt like a groupie meeting their rock-star idol. *I'll never wash that hand again.* Another part was a little more confident: I pictured myself standing in that same spot in a few short years, greeting another wide-eyed youngster who would look at me with the same amount of admiration. I felt it was my destiny.

I didn't realise it at the time, but a lot of things need to fall into place before you get the chance to play for Australia. Talent, hard work and luck are just some of them. Choosing the right sport is another.

I was built like a one-wood as a kid. Big head, long, skinny body. It's a tribute to the wonderful sport of rugby that it had a place for me at all. Looking back, I didn't have enough talent and was way too soft. I was never big enough to make it as a second rower (the men who provide the power in the scrum) and never fast enough to play in the back row (a position in which you run at speed all game to make sure your team keeps possession). But I was tall, so I did OK, which gave me false hope.

I made a couple of junior representative teams and came tantalisingly close to achieving my dream, albeit at an age-group level, when I was named a shadow member of the Australian Under 17s rugby team. This basically meant that if one of the 90-kilogram second rowers selected ahead of me injured themselves, the 75-kilogram sapling that was Mick Colliss would have been called up. I remember training like a maniac on the off-chance their bad luck would be my good fortune, but it wasn't to be.

Still, it gave me a glimpse of being in a rep team and I liked what I saw. I also liked the gear that went with it: kit bag, shoes, boots, jersey, shorts, socks, blazer, pants, tie, jumper, T-shirt, sloppy joe and tracksuit. All embroidered with the Australian coat of arms. It was like getting a whole new wardrobe where everything matched.

I progressed through the system and, in 1986, won the Bryan Palmer Shield for being the 'Most Outstanding Colt'. A guy by the name of Richard Harry was runner-up. He went on to play thirty-seven tests for Australia. In Perth, my second row partner at university was a prodigous talent by the name of John Welborn. John became WA's first home-grown Wallaby when he ran on against the Springboks in

1996 to play the first of his six tests. It was hard not to be encouraged by my team mates' success, so I continued pushing myself to make the most of my meagre talents. I felt that I was mixing in the right circles and was on the right path. It was only a matter of time before the gods of sport smiled and pointed their gnarled fingers at me.

When you're a young kid and obsessed with sport like I was, meeting first graders is a real thrill. I remember in Year 12 we had to fill out a form on which one of the questions was: 'What do you want to do when you leave school?' I wrote, 'Play first grade.' To me, first graders were only one step away from the internationals that I wanted to be.

Steve Cutler, from the Gordon club, will go down in history as one of Australian rugby's greatest second rowers. Over two metres tall and weighing 117 kilograms, he was a massive human being, but his height and accompanying long legs, and the short shorts of the day, made him look lanky – almost awkward.

He made his test debut in 1982 but it wasn't till 1984, in the home series against the All Blacks, that he established himself as one of the stars on the international scene. His lineout play was outstanding and he proved to be the difference between the two sides. He copped a hammering from the physical New Zealanders but refused to be intimidated.

As a young, lanky, awkward-looking second rower myself, I quickly adopted the man known as 'Skylab' as my idol. I even started wearing the same green and yellow striped electrical tape over my ears as Steve did.

A few years later, I played against him in a pre-season trial game at Eastwood's TG Milner Field. It was my first year out of Colts and I was over the moon. I stood next to him in the lineout and couldn't believe I was actually jumping against Steve Cutler. I knew it was one of those moments I'd tell my grandkids about. We were defending twenty metres out from our line and it was a Gordon throw. This was in the days before lifting in lineouts, so there were no fancy moves to try to counter. The ball was going either to the number-two or number-four jumper.

I was waiting and watching, trying to pick up some sort of signal as to where it might end up. I tracked the ball as it left the hooker's hands. It was going to four. To Steve Cutler. This was my moment. My chance to impress Steve. To impress the selectors. To win one against Australia's greatest-ever lineout exponent. I jumped. Gave it everything I had. A mass of arms reached to the sky, like some sort of acrobatic octopus, and the ball was knocked to the ground. I'd managed to spoil the Gordon throw. I was feeling quietly pleased with myself. Then, WHACK. My idol punched me in the head and scowled, 'Don't jump on my feet again.'

I was heartbroken. Almost feeling like I should say, *I'm sorry, Mr Cutler. I didn't mean it.* Play moved on, Steve moved on. But I just stood there, trying to comprehend what had happened. My greatest moment had disintegrated before my eyes. I felt empty.

It was only a trial match, so Steve was replaced at the end of the first half. I don't remember how long I lasted; I was rattled and never recovered. I should have followed Steve's example in that game against the All Blacks and just kept going. But I didn't. I couldn't. It wasn't physical pain, it was mental pain. So I did what any other sensitive New Age rugby forward would have done.

I found a substitute for Steve Cutler.

Steve Williams, Cutler's Wallaby second-row partner from the Manly club, became my new idol. And I never spoke of the Cutler moment again.

It always surprises me when I hear sportsmen say they don't want to be role models. They just are, whether they like it or not. Why wouldn't an impressionable boy want to be what they are and do what they do? The influence they have is beyond anything they could imagine.

One of my fondest memories is of something that happened while I was with other players from the Eastwood rugby club, delivering phone books to houses in Dundas, a leafy, middle-class suburb in Sydney's north west. Rugby in those days was strictly amateur and this was an annual fundraising event for the club. Mid-way through the morning, Ian Williams, the first-grade winger, was tracked down by his father and told to go and make a phone call. (This was how things worked before mobiles.) Ian left us, then returned an hour or so later to announce he'd been picked for the Wallabies.

That was a huge moment for me – I can't fathom how huge it must have been for him. He had brought a case of beer back with him, so we all stopped, used the *White Pages* as makeshift chairs in the tray of the ute and toasted his great news.

I felt like I was closer than ever to my dream.

In 1989, I watched the Wallabies play the British Lions at the Sydney Football Stadium. As always, the national anthem was played before kick off. Only this time the words were displayed on the big screen. The crowd belted out the song like never before. It was amazing. Instead of a few hundred people mumbling their way through, 40,000 voices as one reverberated around the ground, each person encouraging the other to sing louder. It makes my hair stand on end just thinking about it.

It also made me feel even prouder to be Australian and more determined than ever to be one of the players out on the ground listening to that magical sound. I can't imagine what it must be like to stand out there, arm in arm with your team before a test match, singing the anthem in front of a packed house.

John Eales, the great Wallaby captain and second rower, used to pick out someone in the crowd and sing the anthem to them. He said it helped him realise how lucky he was to be playing for his country, knowing how much that person would love to be in his shoes. Obviously, he picked me out more than once.

After my Sydney Football Stadium experience, I couldn't wait for the next time I could sing 'Advance Australia Fair' at the top of my voice. It's not that I was blessed vocally – far from it – I just enjoyed singing that song. Every time I did, I imagined I was about to play a test match for Australia at one of the famous grounds such as Twickenham in England or Cardiff Arms Park in Wales. I used to love watching on TV the games played there and listening to the instant choirs that would form in the grandstands. I'd watch tears roll down the players' cheeks when they sang their anthems before the game. Oh, how I wished that were me…

Rugby test matches didn't take place in Perth until the late 1990s, so we had to find suitable occasions on which to sing our anthem. I played with a couple of pommy mates who took great delight in singing 'God save our gracious Queen', except they'd point to us and sing 'God save *your* gracious Queen'. Most Saturday nights after rugby became suitable occasions for us to go anthem against anthem, with well-lubricated throats.

One of my favourite haunts is the Ocean Beach Hotel at North Cottesloe in Perth. It's right on the coast and has massive windows that open up to make you feel like you're almost sitting on the sand. Watching the sun set over Rottnest Island from one of the front-row tables is pure joy. One night at closing, my mates and I were feeling decidedly merry and broke into song. After a few initial strange looks, the rest of the crowd joined in. They'd been looking for an opportunity to sing our anthem too. Patriotism was alive and I wanted more of it. Only, I wanted to see it from the inside.

College football is massive in the United States. The annual Rose Bowl attracts close to 100,000 fans and is broadcast across the country. College football is not so big in Australia.

I studied at a teachers' college in Castle Hill in western Sydney, which meant I was eligible to try out for the New South Wales Colleges of Advanced Education (NSWCAE) rugby team. So I did, and I was successful. We wore the sky-blue jersey with the waratah embroidered on the chest. It was a proud moment. We toured Hong Kong and Taiwan, and then played a game against Queensland Colleges, from which an Australian Colleges team was chosen.

This was when the Wallaby team played in the Adidas strip with three green stripes down the arms of a gold jersey and three gold stripes down the sides of green shorts. It remains one of the great playing uniforms. I wasn't selected, but could see the pride in the faces of those who were. I could also see their excitement when they realised that the Australian Colleges kit was the same as the Wallabies', albeit with a different crest.

I made the Australian Colleges team two years later. By this time, Canterbury had replaced Adidas as the major gear supplier and the Wallaby jersey was plain gold. The powers that be decided that we should wear the opposite colours to the senior Australian team's, so we were presented with green jerseys. Still, an Australian jersey is an Australian jersey. I was happy and proud, but had a long way to go.

Adrian McDonald, the reserve Wallaby half-back in 1983 and a member of the 1991 World Cup squad, spent some of his career at Eastwood. He mentioned to me that he'd seen my name in the results section of the paper when the team was announced and he offered his congratulations. I was quite sheepish, almost embarrassed by his good wishes. He was a fantastic player and a genuine Wallaby, someone I admired immensely. I said, 'It's only colleges.' To which he replied, 'Yeah, but you're still representing Australia.'

He was a kindred spirit.

CHAPTER 2
Lawn Bowls

When my fortieth birthday was closer than my thirtieth, I realised that my dream of playing for Australia at the highest level was on life support. I was way past my best, which was mediocre on a good day, in all the sports I had ever tried.

Like many who shared my dream, my thoughts turned to the only real option remaining. Lawn bowls. For years I had told myself that when all other avenues had been exhausted, I'd take up bowls and play for Australia. My grandfather played first-grade rugby league in Sydney and was a good lawn bowler, so maybe this was where the genes would kick in. With a bit of luck, they'd get me all the way to the Commonwealth Games.

I visited Claremont Bowling Club in Perth on an Open Day to see if I had the necessary skill set. It was everything I had expected – quiet, like a living time capsule from the 1950s, with great characters who were full of great stories. Our society tends to ignore senior citizens, but they have so much experience and knowledge to share with younger generations. We should introduce an 'Adopt a Grandparent' scheme, in which young people can go to their local bowlo and get partnered with a senior citizen. They can sit with them, share a drink, slow down and shoot the breeze for a few hours. They'd get so much out of it.

I'm not the fastest learner, but after three consecutive weekends of roll-ups and calls of 'good grass skip', it was clear even to me that there's more to being a good lawn bowler than just being old. When it's forty-two degrees in the middle of a Perth summer and you're being beaten by 80-year-old ladies, it doesn't take long for the penny to drop. You accept your fate, put the jack back in the bag, your tail between your legs and head to the beach.

Just like Grant Kenny.

He's another person who had inspired me to chase my dreams. I sat in front of an old black-and-white TV set in 1980 and watched the man who would later become the face of Nutri-Grain breakfast cereal win the junior and senior Australian surf lifesaving iron man titles within an hour of each other. I was obviously very impressionable because, from that day, I wanted to be an iron man.

Ten years later (before my illustrious lawn bowls career), I was. Not a very good one, but an iron man just the same. It was a slight deviation from the road to playing for Australia, but I felt I was more physically suited to surf than to rugby and dared to think I might actually do okay. There was an Australian surf-lifesaving team, and Grant had gone on to represent his country paddling kayaks at the Olympics.

Maybe I'd found my niche.

My first race was the Scarborough leg of the now defunct Kelloggs Nutri-Grain Iron Man Series. All the big names were there, including Darren and Dean Mercer, dual Australian iron man champion Robert Chapman, Jonathan Crowe and a host of other highly talented, extremely fit athletes. I was well out of my league and was never going to win, or even be any sort of competition, but it was the start of my career, so I knew my limitations and was happy just to be there. I figured my ability would allow me to stay up the back, learn and follow everyone else around the course.

Nice idea in principle.

By the time the race started, the sea breeze was in. The dreaded Freo Doctor, as it's known. If you've ever swum in surf when it's windy and there's a swell, you'll understand how hard it is to see anything when you're out in the water in those conditions. I soon became lost. I was 150 metres offshore and thinking, 'How embarrassing. I'm supposed to be an iron man and I'll need to be rescued.' I hadn't listened carefully to the course instructions because I was just going to follow everyone else. So I was out the back, with no idea which buoy to swim to or around. Luckily, some patrolling surf lifesavers in a rubber duckie pointed me and another competitor in the right direction and we made it back to the beach.

That's probably why lawn bowls seemed such a good option, despite the hot weather. At least it was on dry land. And I had a good twenty years to sharpen my skills and force my way into the national team. Being a rookie at sixty sounded perfect. Then I discovered the horrible truth. Elite lawn bowls is not an old man's game. Far from it. It's a game dominated by kids like Mark Berghofer, a member of the Australian lawn bowls team at the age of just twenty-three. I was glad I wasn't female because the situation with the Australian women's team is even more disheartening: Kelsey Cottrell is only eighteen.

Not even the ice-cold, wallet-friendly seven-ounce beers and triangle sandwiches were enough to keep me interested in lawn bowls.

For the next few years, I accepted my place in society and refrained from tormenting myself about representing this great country of ours. Instead, I decided to ride the coat tails of friends who were doing it.

I first met Marty Roebuck when I was seventeen. We lived together for a number of years and became great mates. We were best men at each other's weddings. Part of our bond was the desire to play rugby at the highest level. We trained hard and often, but history will show that only one of us went on to play fullback for the Wallabies and win a gold medal at the 1991 rugby World Cup.

Marty presented me with one of his Wallaby jerseys — the sacred cloth. I felt honoured. I couldn't help but try it on once when I was alone. It looked good and felt good, but I never did it again. I felt like an impostor. Next time I tried on a jersey, it would have to be one of my own.

I would have married Marty if I'd been that way inclined, but I ended up marrying into Australian sporting royalty of another kind. Sharan Wheelock (she only uses my name when she's writing cheques or using our credit card) played water polo for Australia for nine seasons. She competed in two world championships and three world cups, winning gold in 1995. She was vice captain between 1996 and 1998 and captained Australia in a series against Greece in the lead-up to the 1998 World Swimming Championships in Perth.

Once again, I was mixing in the right circles. But I was stranded, hovering on the fringes of national selection without ever making it myself.

The closest I ever got was when I had the rare honour of being the liaison officer for the Dutch women's water polo team at the World Swimming Championships in 1998. My role was to make sure the team had everything they needed, so all they had to worry about was the competition. If there was a problem, I'd fix it. If they wanted to know where to go for dinner, I'd tell them. If they wanted to go sightseeing, I'd organise it.

Being surrounded by a team of fit, healthy, attractive female athletes was quite intimidating. But I took my role seriously and made sure I was on hand to help in anyway I could. After meeting the team at the airport, I ensured they arrived at their hotel safely and checked in without any dramas. The next day, we had a training session booked at the outdoor water-polo pool at Challenge Stadium in Perth, the venue for the tournament.

They had come from winter in Holland, and Perth was in great form, with scorching hot days and cloudless blue skies. All the players were keen to take home a dark tan as a souvenir but I was scared to be anywhere that I might cast a shadow. All those skin cancer warnings I'd been exposed to were obviously sinking in.

Europeans are a lot more comfortable with nudity than Australians are. That was the first thing I discovered. After a solid, blow-the-cobwebs-out training session, the girls changed out of their one-piece water-polo costumes into bikinis. Right in front of me. It took me completely by surprise. Everywhere I looked there was bosom and fur. A temporary grandstand was under construction at the time and I've never seen tradesmen move so quickly from one end of a work site to the other, just so they could get a better view.

I didn't know whether to stand my ground or move away, so I decided to err on the side of caution and slowly made my way to the opposite end of the pool. Like all good liaison officers, I kept my eye on the team and noticed that the bikinis were also being worn as a one piece, with most tops being left in the kit bag.

Just then, the team manager called me over. My immediate thought was that I was making the girls uncomfortable by hanging around, albeit at a safe distance. Instead, I was handed a pile of player profile sheets to distribute. I just stood there.

'Can you give these out, please?' was the request.

'Now?' came my reply.

I took the look of confusion on the team manager's face as a yes, so started heading back towards the girls, who were by now either sitting up chatting or lying on their backs. Many of them still wearing only one half of a bikini.

With my eyes directed towards the sky, frightened to look anywhere else for fear of being branded a pervert on my first full day, I handed out the forms, one by one. I'm sure the players wondered what the hell I was doing. Even when they thanked me, I couldn't bring myself to lower my eye line. The only faces I saw belonged to the tradesmen high up in the grandstand. Tradesmen with watermelon smiles, who'd decided that 10.30am was as good a time as any for a lunch break.

It was a wonderful experience and a real privilege to be welcomed into the inner sanctum of a senior national team at such a prestigious event. I can't speak highly enough of the girls or of their management and I was incredibly sad when my tenure ended. I had gone to training with the team, to the games, I ate with them and relaxed with them for two whole weeks. They made me feel so welcome. I even became comfortable with the nudity. Being their liaison officer was one of the highlights of my life, the closest I had ever been to being part of a national team.

It was everything I had hoped it would be. And I loved it.

CHAPTER 3

What's Sudoku?

There are five seasons every year. Spring, summer, autumn, winter and rugby. The highlight of the latter is the representative program involving the Wallabies playing a series of domestic test matches.

Every year, a group of mates and I try to travel interstate to watch Australia play. There is now an annual Wallabies game in Perth but it's played at Subiaco Oval, the home ground of the West Coast Eagles AFL team. Subi Oval is a great venue, as long as you're not there to watch rugby. You're just too far from the action and you spend more time watching the game on the big screen.

Suncorp Stadium in Queensland is the exact opposite. There are no bad seats at Suncorp. You can hear the lineout calls, hear the hits, smell the liniment. You feel you're part of it.

When we heard the Wallabies were due to play the All Blacks at Suncorp, we decided Brisbane would be our destination for the year. We booked our flights, arranged our accommodation and began counting down the days.

I'm just shy of six foot five on the old scale, so economy seating and I are not the greatest combination. One member of the tour party is Mark 'Skiffo' Skiffington, a wonderful mate, with whom I played rugby for many years. A powerful, hard-running centre, he regularly tops the scales at more than 100 kilograms. Why we sit together on long flights remains a mystery, but we do.

We were an hour out of Perth en route to sunny Brisvegas. My cramped legs were numb with pins and needles and the person in front of me had their seat fully reclined. My extended tray table was pushing my stomach hard up against my spine. It was nearly cutting me in half. Skiffo and I are both borderline homophobes but we'd accepted the fact we'd be touching arms for the next four hours.

There was a problem with the inflight movie, so Skiffo wrenched a buttock clear of the arm rest and bent forward to reach into his travel bag. I took the opportunity to raise my left arm out and away from my body to encourage circulation in my upper torso. When he leant back, I noticed he was holding a book of sudoku puzzles.

'What's that?' I asked.

'Sudoku,' came the reply.

For the next fifteen minutes I watched my companion, pencil in hand, scribble then erase numbers from a series of squares. I was amazed by what I saw.

'How does it work?'

His reply was as precise as his technique: 'Each puzzle is made up of a nine-by-nine grid. Each row and column must contain the numbers one to nine and no number can appear more than once in each row and column.'

It sounded simple enough, so I continued to watch the master at work. Scribbling, erasing, scribbling. Writing small numbers when he wasn't exactly sure. Making them large when he was. Using the given numbers as clues. It's a game of tactics and logic. I was intrigued.

For the next hour and a half, I stared as Skiffo made his way through puzzle after puzzle. He was a genius.

It's funny how the human brain works. When you least expect it, you come up with the most brilliant ideas. It's as though the brain is some sort of industrial-strength oven. You pile a whole lot of thoughts in, then walk away. Days, months, even years later, the brain finishes processing and analysing them and…bing! One freshly baked idea, ready for consumption.

'Skiffo,' I began. 'I was thinking. Why don't we organise a World Sudoku Championship?'

He stopped writing.

'We can pick ourselves in the Australian side. *We can play for Australia.*

'We'll hold it at the rugby club, invite our pommy mates to play for England, the kiwis can play for New Zealand and we'll play against any other nations that turn up.

'And, Skiffo, you can captain Australia.'

It takes a lot to get the big man excited but this struck a chord. Like me, he would have loved to have represented his country. And, again like me, he had thought the chance had passed him by.

The remainder of the flight was spent in animated conversation. Ideas flowed as freely as the Heinekens. For the first time in our lives, we had a real chance of wearing the green and gold.

When we touched down in Brisbane, rugby was the furthest thing from our minds. Watching Australia play wasn't nearly as exciting as playing for Australia. We discussed marketing ideas, media coverage and potential sponsors who would provide important things such as prizes and beer. We even discussed team uniforms. It was all coming together nicely. Sudoku, a game I'd never even heard of less than twenty-four hours earlier, became the topic of a conversation that lasted all weekend. Even the Wallabies losing 13–9 to the All Blacks didn't dampen our spirits.

I don't know why I did it. Curiosity, I guess. When I returned to Perth I googled World Sudoku Championships.

The 1st World Sudoku Championship (WSC1) was held in beautiful Lucca, Italy, on March 10–12, 2006.

I couldn't believe it.

All the excitement, all the enthusiasm, all the pending glory. Over in one fell click of a computer mouse.

The dream was dead. I was back to square one.

CHAPTER 4

Never say never

It took me three goes to get my driver's licence. Two goes to get accepted into the fourth university I attended. Three goes to get my surf lifesaving bronze medallion. Three girlfriends to break my duck. I don't consider myself to be overly determined; I'm certainly not the type who, once I set my mind to something, will do anything and everything to make sure I achieve it. But I am persistent.

I watched a lot of TV growing up, which meant I watched a lot of ads. Most of them were pretty ordinary and I thought I could do better. So when I was given the chance in Year 10 to do work experience, I thought I'd try advertising. I knew nothing about the industry and didn't know anyone involved in it but thought I'd like to write TV commercials. I pulled out the *Yellow Pages*, looked up 'Advertising Agencies' and sent out a few letters asking if they'd take me on for a couple of weeks.

The response was amazing. Overwhelming. Not a single reply. Not even a rejection letter. So I thought, 'Right, advertising can get fucked.' If they didn't want anything to do with me, I didn't want anything to do with them.

I still had to do work experience somewhere, so with time running out, I called up a mate's dad and ended up doing a two-week stint with the Department of Main Roads. I was allocated to a road gang and spent my time putting out witches hats in preparation for road works, hammering wooden pegs for the surveyors and going to the pub for lunch.

The guys I worked with were good lads but not the brightest of bulbs. During one of our regular smokos I was sitting down eating a sandwich when one of the guys asked his mate if he'd seen *The Postman Always Rings Twice*, a movie that had recently been released. His mate replied, 'No, I haven't even seen it once yet.' I was giggling to myself, thinking these blokes are actually quite witty and sharp. Until the first guy said, deadpan: 'No, that's what the movie is called.'

Another time, I was in the lunchroom back at the depot during a morning-tea break. The foreman was perched in front of a small TV watching *Wonder Woman*. The reception was terrible. The image was blurry and the ghosting was so bad that each character had a double. When one of the guys asked why he didn't adjust the aerial, another explained that the foreman liked it that way because he got to see Wonder Woman with four tits.

Those were the days.

While I had vowed never to have anything to do with advertising, I still enjoyed writing, so when I left school a couple of years later, I thought I'd become a journalist. I enrolled in a Bachelor of Arts course, majoring in Communications, at Sydney's Macquarie University. I spent the first year doing a variety of subjects that had nothing to do with writing. I was doing psychology, linguistics, a couple of education units and even an electronics unit. Apparently, the first-year subjects are supposed to help you decide what you really want to do. I thought I knew what I wanted to do, which was why I chose the course in the first place. At the end of the year, I spoke to one of the lecturers and said that I wanted to be a journalist. His response was that I wouldn't learn any writing in the course I was doing.

So I quit.

I'm sure he won't remember it, but the person I sat with in lectures during that first year at Macquarie Uni was a guy called Peter Overton. Pete ended up working as a journalist and reporter on Channel Nine's flagship *60 Minutes* program. Maybe I should have stuck with the BA.

I liked sport, so applied to study phys ed teaching the following year. The phys ed course was great. There were only about twenty students in my year and we all shared the same interests. This was a refreshing change from some of my tutorial groups at Macquarie Uni, which were dominated by man-hating lesbians in khaki bib-and-brace overalls.

When I finished my diploma, I moved to Perth to get my degree at the University of Western Australia. UWA's Human Movement Department had an international reputation and was very much geared towards corporate health and fitness, as opposed to teaching in schools. I was sharing a place with two other mates from Sydney who'd joined me on the trek across the Nullarbor and, like most students, none of us had much more than the clothes on our backs as far as material possessions were concerned.

I needed to get a part-time job in order to survive and was very fortunate to land one as a fitness instructor at the head office of Woodside Offshore Petroleum in Perth. This was one of Australia's best corporate facilities, so I was extremely grateful for the opportunity. I even managed to get a couple of trips out to the oil rig, located off Australia's north-west shelf. Standing on the helideck, turning 360 degrees and seeing nothing but ocean and horizon, was amazing.

When I finished my degree, my part-time position became full-time and, with my new-found knowledge, I started writing articles for various health and fitness magazines. It was something I enjoyed doing, and after a couple of years, studying journalism was back on my radar. So I applied to do a graduate diploma in English, majoring in journalism, at Curtin University. Despite having articles published and a monthly column in a lifestyle magazine, I didn't get in. I tried again the following year and that time the decision went in my favour.

It was my sixth year of study and one of my most enjoyable. Due to all the other courses I'd done, I was given a lot of credits and only had to do the core units – writing for TV, radio and newspapers. No electronics, psychology or Rwandan basket-weaving. The gym sessions I had been doing were mainly outside normal office hours, so I was able to combine a full-time job with full-time study.

Eventually, though, the long days and constant rushing from work to uni and back to work again began to take its toll. Something had to give. Luckily, the decision was made for me when Woodside underwent cutbacks and the fitness centre's budget, along with my working hours, were greatly reduced.

The timing was actually quite good. I was heading off on a university rugby club tour to North America and Canada about a month later, so thought I might as well take advantage of my predicament. I didn't see my future as running fitness centres, so I resigned from what was left of my job and had my last day at the office the day before the tour left. I boarded the plane with a hangover, and pretty much woke up the same way for the next seventeen days.

We played a game in Portland, Oregon, which happens to be where the head office of Wieden+Kennedy, one of advertising's most famous agencies, is located. Wieden+Kennedy began at a kitchen table with one client – a fledgling shoe company called Nike. Agent and client have been together ever since. I was lucky enough to be given a tour and when I walked in I couldn't believe I was in an office. It was more like a sports museum. Everywhere I looked, I saw autographed NFL helmets, basketballs, rugby balls, running shoes and baseballs – literally hundreds of thousands of dollars' worth of sports memorabilia covered the walls, desks and shelves.

I loved sport and enjoyed being creative. Here I was, looking at people who combined the two every day. I forgave advertising in an instant. This was what I wanted to do.

One of the players from the Portland team worked at Wieden+Kennedy, so I spoke to him about getting an internship at the agency. Once again, I was rejected by the industry I was so keen to embrace – this time because I wasn't a US citizen.

I was disappointed but figured it would be a waste not to finish my journalism course when I only had one unit to complete. When the tour officially ended, I sobered up and travelled around Canada for another month or so on borrowed funds, before making my way back to Perth.

I was about to turn twenty-eight. I had no money, no job and no girlfriend. I could have taken any number of actions to remedy my situation – well, the money and job bit of the equation anyway. But what did I do? I decided to give my iron-man career one last crack.

Sensible? No.

Trevor Hendy, the six-times Australian and four-times World Iron Man Champion, ruled the waves and I thought if I used the three-month window before uni started again to train hard, I'd have a fair indication of how good I could possibly be. On paper, Trevor and I were pretty similar. I was slightly taller and a few kilos heavier. Maybe that green and gold blazer wasn't so far out of reach after all.

Delusional? Absolutely.

It was summer, which meant that the sun appeared well before the rest of the city rose from the previous night's sticky slumber. And there's no better place to be when the sun is still stretching and yawning than the beach. It's beautiful first thing in the morning. The changing light bathes the coast in pinky golden hues, while the offshore breeze makes the surface of the ocean smooth. Even the shadows of the buildings on the sand recede like bedcovers, as though the shoreline itself is slowly waking.

There's a real sense of calmness at this time. Then the beach bursts into life from just before six o'clock with people of all ages running, swimming, walking, doing tai chi and generally enjoying the playground we are so blessed to have on our doorstep. By half-past seven, it's virtually deserted again as the morning rush subsides and people head home to prepare for their day ahead.

Swimming, running and paddling at that time of day is almost therapeutic. Occasionally, I've been out on my ski and had the pleasure of following one of the many pods of dolphins that frolic off Perth's beaches. Mind you, that first glimpse of a dark grey fin slicing through the water often had me heading back to the car to change my Speedos. *JAWS* has a lot to answer for. But being so close to one of nature's most graceful animals, in their natural environment, is very humbling.

In my mind, as I was training, I was paddling against Clint Robinson, the Olympic Kayak Gold Medallist from 1992 and the most decorated of all Australian surf lifesavers. I'd picture him just in front of me and try to mirror his flawless technique. I could almost hear him thinking, 'Who's this guy on my wash? Why can't I shake him?' I'd catch a small wave into the beach, make a seamless transition and sprint off on the run leg, imagining I was closing in on the race leaders. Hordes of spectators, all in bikinis and none over the age of twenty-five, were cheering me, my rippling thighs and chiselled torso glistening in the brilliant sunshine.

In reality, my paddling resembled that of a bird with a broken wing, my physique was more David Hasselhoff (circa *Baywatch* season nine) than Adonis, and my run leg made Cliff Young look like Matt Shirvington. But I felt so alive.

It was an idyllic lifestyle but one that needed to be financed. Having no money is something we elite athletes grudgingly accept. It's all part of the sacrifice. We know we'll struggle. But we also know that once we start winning, the lucrative endorsements will start rolling in and we'll look back and laugh at our modest beginnings.

While I had no doubt that a massive sponsorship proposal was just around the corner, I had to find a solution for the here and now, to tide me over until the big bucks arrived. So I took myself off to the local CES to register for the dole. Problem solved. It was only when I handed in my application form that I discovered part of the deal with getting the dole was applying for jobs on a regular basis. I was directed to a large notice board covered in job advertisements and began searching.

It must have been my lucky day because one of the first vacancies I saw was for a writer. That was perfect. I would have felt bad applying for a job as a carpenter or a psychologist, or some other position I knew I wouldn't get. I actually wanted to be a writer, so no one could accuse me of rorting the system. I applied and went for an interview.

And got the job.

I was devastated. The Summer of Mick was over before it began. Trevor Hendy's reign as Australian Iron Man champion would have to continue unchallenged.

The following Monday I packed my lunch and set off for my first day. From 7.30am till 4pm I wore a borrowed tie and sat in a corner writing the messages you hear over the phone when you're put on hold.

It was a long way from the beach.

It's funny how things work out. When I was at Woodside, part of my role was to advertise the various promotions the fitness centre was running. It was my favourite part of the job, so I decided to send a self-promotion flyer out to the main advertising agencies in Perth, asking if they had a position for someone like me. None did, but I received a response from Roger McMillan, the rugby-loving, surf-lifesaving-loving Creative Director of Results, a local advertising and direct-marketing company. He suggested I apply for something called AWARD School, which was a twelve-week course specifically for people wanting to work in the creative department of an advertising agency.

So I applied. And I missed out.

Advertising was really starting to piss me off.

I spent the best part of six months in that job, trying to convince people to 'ask for more details when they come off hold'. That was my life from Monday to Thursday. Friday was my day at uni. When I finally completed my course, I was asked if I'd like to work five days a week writing phone messages. My first reaction was no, but I had appreciated the work while I was studying and thought a bit of goodwill couldn't hurt. That, and the fact that my letterbox wasn't exactly buckling under the strain of job offers flooding in. I was one day away from signing the contract that would make me a forty-hour-a-week on-hold message writer when the call came:

'What are you doing with your life?'

It was Roger.

'Nothing,' came my reply.

'Do you want a job?'

Abbott Mead Vickers BBDO is one of the UK's largest advertising agencies. They won the Guinness account on the back of the slogan 'Good things come to those who wait'. I guess they do. It had taken me thirteen years from the time I first thought about becoming a writer in an advertising agency to being offered the chance to actually be one. Needless to say, I didn't have to be asked twice.

Looking back, getting that job after all those years was a significant moment. It breathed new life into a dream that had almost flickered out. It made me realise that anything was possible. Even representing Australia.

CHAPTER 5

Star Trek and comic books

I consider myself an optimist. Every night, I ask my wife for sex. Every night, she knocks me back. But I keep asking.

When I found out that someone had already set up a World Sudoku Championship, I was disappointed. The glass was definitely half empty. But, when I managed to step back and look at the situation without becoming emotional, I realised that the existence of a World Sudoku Championship actually worked in my favour. Organising the event would have been hard work, but someone had already done it for me. In effect, I was closer than I thought to my dream because I had one less thing to do. Suddenly, the glass was half full.

With renewed enthusiasm, I hopped back on the internet – the horse that had bucked me off just one month earlier. I wanted to know all about the World Sudoku Championship. Who organised it? Who gets to compete? How do you qualify?

I'm not a puzzler – I didn't even know the noun existed. But the longer I looked, the more I learned and the more frightened I became. The puzzling world is huge. Bigger than anything I could have imagined. To put it into perspective, when you google 'Pamela Anderson nude' you get around one and a half million results. Google 'sudoku' and you get more than fifty-eight million. That's how big it is.

My research was a journey into the unknown. I was going where members of my normal social network fear to tread. To a sub-set of human society that's part *Star Trek* convention, part rocket science and part comic-book collector. I was well out of my comfort zone. But I soldiered on. A spot in the Australian team was at stake.

My major breakthrough came with the discovery of the World Puzzle Federation (WPF). According to its own website, the WPF is 'an international organization dedicated to puzzles. It follows the Olympic standard, and brings together puzzlers from around the world for the annual World Puzzle Championship (WPC)'.

The *World* Puzzle Federation. Who'd have thought?

I'm still not sure what is meant by 'Olympic standard', but if the WPF manages to convince Jacques Rogge, the President of the International Olympic Committee, that puzzling should be an Olympic event, I'll be the first to offer my congratulations.

From what I could tell, the WPF is to puzzling what the International Cricket Council (ICC) is to cricket and the International Rugby Board (IRB) is to rugby union. It's the international governing body. As my research continued, I discovered that the WPF is also responsible for the World Sudoku Championship. The second such event, held in Prague, attracted 114 competitors from thirty-four different countries. It was a lot bigger than the one I would have run at our rugby club.

Every country competing at the World Sudoku Championship had a national body representing the WPF, much the same way as the Australian Rugby Union and Australian Cricket Board are the national representatives of their respective international organisations. Each national member of the WPF is responsible for holding their own state and national titles, with the latter acting as the selection trial for the national team to compete at the World Sudoku Championships.

At the US Nationals, nearly a thousand people took part. The winner was Thomas Snyder, a 27-year-old postdoctoral student in bioengineering at Stanford University. Snyder's victory not only secured his spot in the American team, it added $10,000 to his bank balance.

This was serious stuff. And so it should be.

By nature, Australians are a fairly adventurous bunch. The 'have-a-go' attitude is something for which we've always been famous. Arrive at some out-of-the-way location that no one's ever heard of, and chances are you'll hear an Australian accent before the day is out. So you can imagine my surprise when I scanned the alphabetical listing of participating countries at the 2nd World Sudoku Championship and went from Argentina straight to Austria.

There was no Australian team.

Maybe we'd had a bad run of injuries. I continued searching and found the list of national WPF members. Once again, Australia's name was missing.

I kept trying to make sense of everything. Then the penny dropped. There was no Australian team at the World Sudoku Championship because Australia wasn't a member of the WPF.

It was then I realised that I had stumbled upon one of those once-in-a-lifetime opportunities.

What if I applied? What if *I* became Australia's member of the WPF?

For the first time in a long time, I did something useful with my right hand. I grabbed that computer mouse and made it work harder than it ever had before. I read every page of the WPF website. I read the 'How to join' and then the 'Why join?' sections. And there it was, point three, confirmation in black and white:

The benefits of membership include the right to send a team to the World Sudoku Championship.

Could this really be happening? Surely there are terms and conditions. Things like this don't happen to me.

I went back to the 'How to join' section and re-read the key points. To become a national member of the WPF you are supposed to be heavily involved in puzzling. Which I wasn't. I hadn't even attempted a sudoku puzzle. But one sentence stood out:

Membership can be possible without meeting these criteria, but only as long as there are no applicants from the same country meeting all these criteria.

It seemed like a long shot, but if I was the only applicant, membership of the WPF was possible. And if I was the member, it would be my job to pick the Australian team. I quickly sent off for an application form and waited for a response. When I got one from the WPF General Secretary, the news wasn't good.

Dear Mick,

Thank you for showing interest, but Australia is on the brink of already being represented.

Damn it.

As it turned out, the application from one of Australia's largest puzzling companies had already been approved by the WPF board. The only reason they weren't listed on the website was because their membership fee hadn't been paid.

I'd come too far to let the dream go, so in desperation I emailed straight back. The other company had its headquarters on the central coast of New South Wales. I was in Perth, 4000 kilometres away. Could I be the member for Western Australia?

Once again, I waited. And, once again, the answer I received wasn't the one I wanted. The rules were clear – there could only be one member from each country.

I was surprisingly calm when I realised that my dream of playing for Australia was over. Again. It happened so suddenly. Maybe I was in shock. I know I was numb. It didn't seem real. But it was.

CHAPTER 6
It's a boy

Being present at the birth of your child is supposed to be one of life's greatest, most amazing, magical, brilliant, unforgettable moments. I found it to be one of life's most distressing.

As with most things I go into, I had no idea what to expect when it came to the whole pregnancy thing. As far as I knew, you have lots of sex, your partner gets pregnant, becomes the designated driver because she can't drink, she has the child, you bring it home and watch it grow up to play for the Wallabies.

Piece of cake.

When Sharan and I made the decision to have a child, I saw only positives. Especially the sex. I honestly thought I might get on a bit of a roll in that department. String a few wins together. Maybe even get to do it every day. I had a crack on the morning she was leaving on a two-week water polo trip. We did the test when she returned because she had a 'gut feeling'. Sure enough, she was pregnant. I was one from one. Batting 1000. So much for improving my once-a-month average.

As the pregnancy progressed, we went along to a couple of maternity classes. This involved sitting on large balls, something I was quite used to. We also practised our breathing. I had thought I had that pretty much under control, so I was pleasantly surprised to learn about the secret 'pregnancy breathing'. You can never have too many skills.

A couple of months out from the big day, we were given a tour of the hospital. The birthing suite was nice – it was a spacious single room with a TV, cupboard and fridge. I had visions of kicking back with a cold can of Coke, watching the match of the round while my wife did all the work. We also had a look at the spa, which was available to help ease the pain of the contractions. Everything was in order and I felt ready.

All the reading material stressed the importance of having a bag packed well in advance. The theory behind it is that when it's time to go to the hospital, the last thing you want to be thinking about is getting some clothes and toiletries together. That makes sense. I know, because we didn't do it. As soon as her waters broke, I shoved Sharan straight in the car and sped off. We arrived at the hospital and the first question the nurses asked was, 'Do you have a bag with your clothes and toiletries?'

I made up some story about leaving it in the car and continued telling it while they took Sharan off to get examined. Apparently, the mother-to-be has to be dilated a certain number of centimetres before the staff get serious and start preparing for the birth. I tried not to think about the implications of dilation.

Sharan's a fairly hard unit. I'd watched her train for many years, putting up with the pain required to compete at the elite level. She never complained once. She just got in there and did the hard work.

When the contractions started coming, she was okay.

She certainly wasn't out to try to impress anyone, but in the early stages, she could handle the pain and knocked back the offer for drugs.

Then it all started getting a bit ugly.

As the contractions became more regular, the pain increased. To watch someone you love in so much agony is an awful experience. And there's nothing you can do about it. You just have to stand there and look on helplessly as she roams the corridors of the hospital, doubling up in pain every minute.

We remembered the spa, so filled it up and hopped in. Then hopped straight out again. A woman in labour is like a woman in a very bad mood. She's edgy and looking for someone to blame. And, generally, it's the person who got them in that predicament in the first place. All the heat and steam of the spa was claustrophobic, so I was told in no uncertain terms to turn it off and get out. It wasn't the 'Girls of the Playboy Mansion' scene I'd envisaged.

As her pain intensified, we went in search of the doctors. Sharan was calm but I was starting to panic. We both wanted drugs but by this stage it was too late. She was fully dilated and it was time to move to stage two. She'd have to tough it out.

I was too stressed and worried about Sharan even to think about the TV. Or the Coke. The nurses were great and took wonderful care of their patient, so at least I knew she was in good hands.

I'd felt useless many times before but this took it to a new level. I stayed up the non-striker's end and did my best to offer an encouraging word or reassuring rub when I thought it was appropriate. Which it rarely was. I know if

I'd had something else to do, like play in a grand final or a test match, Sharan would have preferred I went and did it.

For most of my adult life, I've gone to bed at 9.30pm so I could get up early to train. Sharan's waters had broken mid afternoon. By the time we got to the hospital it was around 5pm The contractions started about seven o'clock and by the time we made it to the birthing suite, it was after midnight.

I'd been up since about 6am, so I was really struggling. I was an emotional wreck after watching Sharan go through so much pain and was eyeing off the bed she was on, wondering if there was any way I could slide on. The harder Sharan pushed, the harder it was for me to stay awake. Finally, at about 2.10am, Matt was born. The nurses wrapped him up and announced, 'It's a boy.'

I did a quick count of his fingers and toes and was asked if I'd like to cut the umbilical cord. I felt obliged because I'd heard all these other stories from gushing dads about how special it is. But for me, it was a fairly overrated process. I don't know how long those cords are, but it felt like Matt was about ten metres away. I grabbed the scissors and cut through gristle. There was nothing magical about it.

Naturally, Sharan was buzzing. I was exhausted. All I wanted to do was go to sleep. Which wasn't exactly what she wanted to hear. She was full of adrenaline, relieved it was all over and on a huge high.

Sharan was moved to the maternity wing with our newborn son, being wheeled around in one of those movable beds. I was so jealous. There was nowhere for me to lie down, so eventually, at about half-past five, I headed home.

As I drove, barely able to keep my eyes open, the event I had just witnessed and been a part of started to sink in. I realised with those three simple words, 'It's a boy', my life had changed forever. I was now a father. I had a son. It was hard to believe.

I knew it would take something very special to beat that moment. I was lucky enough to equal it a couple of years later with the birth of my second son, Ben. I was two from two and still batting 1000. Once again, Sharan went into labour at night but when we got to the hospital, the nurses checked her and she was nowhere near ready to give birth. There was a spare room with two beds, so we both lay down and grabbed a couple of hours sleep.

When we woke the next morning, there had been no real progress, so I decided to head home for a shower and some breakfast. No sooner had I walked in the door, than my phone rang. It was Sharan, telling me to get back to the hospital. I thought I had at least a few hours, so took my time. When I arrived again, she was already in the suite. I'd had a pretty rough night, being woken up and having to sleep in a bed so short my feet were hanging over the end, so while Sharan was starting to push, I started looking for somewhere to sit. The nurse saw me and asked if I was feeling faint and if I needed a hand. I acted tough and assured her I'd be okay. I was too embarrassed to tell her I was just tired, especially while my wife was in the process of giving birth less than a metre away.

As far as memorable occasions go, the birth of my two boys is right up there with Yvette Higgins scoring the winning goal for the Australian women's water polo team at the Sydney Olympics with less than a second left on the clock, and Totai Kefu scoring the winning try against the All Blacks in John Eales's last test for the Wallabies.

And now it's right up there with an unexpected email I received from the WPF General Secretary, about a month after that last disappointing piece of correspondence:

Hi Mick,

The other company withdrew after all, so the application is open again!

I'm a big believer in fate. And I think if you want to do something, you'll put yourself in a position where it's more likely to happen. That's not to say I believe those people who say if you want something badly enough you'll get it. Far from it. Desire definitely plays a role but you also need lots of luck and lots of talent. Some people are naturally smarter, bigger, faster and stronger. That's just the way it is. If you don't have the raw talent to begin with, you'll struggle. But when everything else is equal, wanting something more than the next person does make a difference.

I had a burning desire to play for Australia. But I knew I'd never achieve the goal with talent alone. I wasn't good enough at anything I tried. So I had to apply my theory and put myself in a position where it was more likely to happen. Then I'd have to rely on a whole lot of luck.

The day that email arrived was the day I got lucky.

I filled in the form and, as requested, wrote a few lines about my organisation and my plans in the field of puzzles. I was working as a creative writer in an advertising agency then and my responses remain some of my best work. My application would be forwarded to the board for approval, then, if it was successful, it was just a matter of paying the 250 euro fee.

Every day for the next month, I checked my email. It was a bit like watching a horror film. I wanted to see, but I didn't want to see, in case the news was bad. Finally, the return email arrived. This was it. I'd spent the last forty years wanting to play for Australia. The email I was about to read would either make or break me. I held my breath and clicked.

Hi Mick,

Just returned from the World Puzzle Championships in Bulgaria, where we had a board meeting. I am happy to be able to tell you that your application has been approved.

Welcome aboard!

I'd done it. I was Australia's member of the World Puzzle Federation. More importantly, I was the sole selector for the Australian team at the next World Sudoku Championship.

For once, my destiny was in my hands. It was a beautiful feeling.

CHAPTER 7

Conditions apply

One of my favourite Henry Lawson short stories is titled 'Two Dogs and a Fence'. It's a wonderfully simple tale of observation, questioning why two dogs, when separated by a fence, become aggressive, barking and acting like they want to rip each other's throats out. If the fence wasn't there, they'd act completely differently.

And Lawson is spot on. If there was no fence, they'd be friendly and polite, greeting each other as only dogs can:

'Hey, how's it going?'

'Yeah, good. And you?'

'Yeah, good thanks.'

'Gee, your bum smells good today.'

'I know. I've just finished rubbing it on the lawn.'

That was how I was feeling. I'd been angry, snarling and growling all my life, unable to play for Australia due to a different kind of barrier – a lack of talent. But, all of a sudden, the fence was gone. I had my chance and I didn't know what to do with it. I'd been chasing the dream for so long I'd almost forgotten what I was chasing it for.

Having said that, I was very excited about being an official Australian selector. I was up there with Allan Border and Bob Fulton, two legends of Australian sport who had had the same job for our national cricket and rugby league teams. I was a man of power.

This might come as a surprise, but there's not really a lot to do when you're the sole selector of the Australian sudoku team. There are no meetings to attend, no phone calls to make, no autographs to sign. Apart from the intrinsic glory and prestige, it's actually quite a lonely position.

Sometimes success isn't all it's cracked up to be.

Although, when my name was finally posted on the WPF website as the Australian member, I did get a couple of emails from people – obviously impressed by my status – asking me to try some of the new puzzles they'd invented and provide some feedback. They said they'd value my opinion.

If only they knew.

One of the required duties of every WPF member was to organise a national sudoku championship. From this, they'd select a national team to compete at the World Championship. That was fine, except I had no idea how to do it. I didn't even know how to organise a local sudoku competition, let alone something involving people from all over the country. Did a group of people sit in a room, start a puzzle and then raise their hand once they'd finished? What if two people raised their hands at the same time? Did you need a video ref to decide? What if the first person who raised their hand made a mistake? The more I thought about it, the more stressed I became.

I don't hate my job. I actually quite like it. But I'd prefer not having to work at all. There are better things I could do with my time. That's why I often have a punt on Lotto when the big prizes are on offer. I don't play when there's only eight or so million up for grabs. I come out of the woodwork when it gets up around thirty million. It's as though eight million isn't enough.

Eight million would, in fact, be more than enough. Three million too many by my calculations. I've always said if someone gave me five million dollars, I'd retire. I'd spend two million on a house and maybe a hundred grand on two new cars. The remaining 2.9 million would go into my bank account. At eight per cent interest, I'd earn $232,000 a year. That's well over twice our current family income and I wouldn't have to leave home to earn it. If I lived how I'm living now in terms of spending, and didn't have to worry about a mortgage, that would leave me a surplus of about $150,000 each year. I could have a luxury family holiday in Bali for two weeks, staying in a five star hotel, for about $6000. I could take a couple of mates and their families with me and still have about $120,000 left over.

Whistler in Canada is beautiful and a fantastic destination if you like skiing. I could book a couple of bungalows in the snow and take my family and friends. We could do a month over the Christmas school holidays. That would probably set me back about fifty grand. That still leaves me with $70,000.

I'd like to think I'd give some to a charity and set up a number of sports scholarships to help cover the costs of training and tours for talented kids from underprivileged families. I'd throw in airfares for the parents too, so they could go and watch their kids compete at major competitions. I'd also like to keep about ten grand up my sleeve to fly a few of my mates business class to watch the Wallabies.

And the best thing is, I wouldn't have touched my 2.9 million in savings, which means I'd get the same 'salary' the next year.

I can't understand it when people who are extremely well off — and I'm talking those with ten million plus — keep working long hours when they don't need to. Maybe they love what they're doing and the money isn't a motivating factor. Or maybe the thrill of making money is an addiction. I wouldn't know, but I'd be happy to find out. At least until I have my five mill.

When I started thinking about organising sudoku competitions as part of my role with the WPF, I toyed with the thought of making it my career. I met a guy in France during the 2007 Rugby World Cup who made his fortune selling padlocks to mine sites. Being a professional sudokuist might not have been as silly as it sounded.

Maths has never been my strong point but if I kept the numbers basic, even I could see there was a dollar to be made. In theory anyway. If I organised the Western Australian State Sudoku Championship, I could aim for 200 competitors and charge them fifty dollars each to enter. That would be $10,000. I could take the same model to New South Wales and Victoria. If I had 300 competitors at fifty dollars each in both of those larger states, that's an extra $30,000. Take my travelling Sudoku State Championships roadshow to the Northern Territory, the ACT, South Australia and Queensland and get 200 competitors each time and my total income for the year is $80,000.

If word spread, I could double the number of competitors the following year and increase the entry fee to sixty dollars, sending my wage rocketing to $192,000. If I could match the efforts of my US counterparts and get 1000 people paying a paltry forty dollars to compete for the title of Australian Champion at the national titles, I'm up to $232,000.

Hello, Bali; hello, Whistler; and hello, Wallabies.

The problem with this plan was my previously mentioned lack of knowledge. When it came to running sudoku competitions, I seriously didn't know where to begin. And if people were paying good money to enter, I wanted to get it right. It wouldn't be fair to stuff it up.

Another problem was that I couldn't afford to quit my job to pursue the dream of organising State Sudoku Championships for a living. Or maybe I just didn't have the guts. I take my hat off to those people who have the balls to sell everything they own and pour all their finances into something they believe in. It must be frightening and exhilarating at the same time.

I've lost three jobs because the companies I worked for fell on hard times. They needed to reduce staff numbers to survive and I was one of the ones 'reluctantly let go'. My last dismissal was particularly tough. I had a twenty-month-old son, my wife was pregnant with our second child and we'd just bought a house we really couldn't afford. To top it off, it was a month until Christmas.

It's not like I wasn't used to being made redundant. But in the past, the only person I had had to worry about was myself. This whole responsibility thing took it to a new level.

I was working in the creative department of a Perth advertising agency that had been around for nearly twenty years. When the owner passed away suddenly, things started going downhill and never recovered. In the end, the agency was simply shut down. A few of us could see the writing on the wall and decided that if things did go wrong, we'd start our own company.

As it happened, things did go wrong.

I remember going home to my wife on the day I was told I was out of a job. 'Sharan,' I said. 'I've got some bad news and some good news. The bad news is, I lost my job today.'

Her reaction was what you'd expect from someone who'd just paid above the odds for a new house and was only a few weeks away from child number two.

'The good news is, I've got another one.'

As I watched the colour return to Sharan's face, I couldn't bring myself to tell her my new job was with an agency that didn't have a name, didn't have an office and didn't have any clients.

As had Wieden+Kennedy, we started our new venture around a kitchen table. Unfortunately, that's where the similarities ended.

I didn't earn a cent for three months. All my savings were gone and I was getting desperate. We cut back on all the luxuries, which meant no more takeaway meals and no more outings to anything that had an admission fee. I was distraught when I had to get Foxtel disconnected. Television had been my rock for so long that I felt like I was deserting one of my best friends.

It got to the point that if I didn't earn something by the end of the next month, I'd have no choice but to rent out our home and move in with my mother-in-law. She's a lovely lady, but I'm sure she was as keen for that to happen as I was.

Thankfully, some money started dribbling in. It wasn't much, but it was enough to meet the bare costs of a mortgage and food. They were scary times. It wasn't a pleasant experience when it was forced on me. It's not the sort of thing I'd like to force on myself.

When someone you know buys a new car, you suddenly see that same model everywhere you go. It was the same with sudoku. I'd never noticed it before but as soon as I became the national selector, I saw it everywhere. People were doing the puzzles on buses, at the beach, at the pool, at cafes. It was like the hula-hoop and yoyo craze all over again. I even went as far as to ask one poor unsuspecting soul who was playing sudoku at the pool if he'd consider paying fifty dollars to enter the West Australian State Sudoku Championship. He looked at me strangely before politely declining on the grounds that he wasn't good enough.

I didn't dare tell him that ability wouldn't be a prerequisite.

Sudoku is a game of logic. The number of toys we have at home defies it. It's ridiculous. Cars, action figures without heads, board games with pieces missing, empty boxes reminding me of what the product should look like, swords, guns, balls, racquets, kites without string, plastic horses without tails. The majority haven't been played with for years. But if I threaten to give them away or throw them out, all hell breaks loose. Similarly, if there are fifty toys spread around my loungeroom floor and one of my kids picks one up, the other child wants that toy. For no other reason than to stop the other from having it.

I was beginning to feel the same way with my WPF membership. As long as I coughed up my 250 euro, I would be the man. No one could compete for Australia at the World Sudoku Championships without my authorisation. I knew I'd struggle to organise the type of competition that was expected of someone in my position but that didn't matter. It was like I wanted the title just so no one else could have it. The realisation that I was being greedy didn't sit too comfortably with me.

Plus there was another problem.

I'm extremely fortunate to have been to some beautiful places in the world. Switzerland is stunning, Queenstown has a fantastic village atmosphere, Bali is perfect for switching off and Paris is magnifique for so many reasons. India, on the other hand, isn't any of those things as far as I was concerned. In all honesty, though, I didn't know anything about it, apart from what I'd seen watching the Australian cricketers play there on TV. My perception was that it was crowded, dirty and if you went there you were guaranteed to get sick.

So I was rather deflated when I heard the subcontinent had been chosen as the venue for the 3rd World Sudoku Championships. If it had been Hawaii or Vancouver or London, I would have been jumping out of my skin with enthusiasm.

But India?

If I was struggling for motivation before, now it was at an all-time low. I just couldn't muster the energy even to find out how to run a national championship.

And that bothered me.

I'd wanted to play for Australia, I'd been given the opportunity and now I was putting conditions on it. I'd turned into one of those horrible retail press ads – FREE PLASMA TV WORTH $999*. When you finally locate the asterisk preceding the fine print at the bottom of the page, you realise the TV is only free if you spend $20,000 on other items of electrical equipment before 5pm that afternoon.

When George Gregan, captain of the Wallabies, withdrew from a tour because he wanted to freshen up for the next lot of games, I couldn't believe it. Same with Ricky Ponting, captain of the Australian cricket team, when he pulled out of a tour. I was the first to rip into them, demanding that they retire. Captaining your country is the greatest honour there is. Would they have pulled out of a tour early on in their career? No way. If captaining Australia has lost its appeal, retire. Get out and give someone who would walk over broken glass for the honour an opportunity.

I was no different. In fact, I was worse. If this was my attitude, I didn't deserve the honour of wearing the green and gold.

CHAPTER 8
Pressure

I'd heard nothing from the World Puzzle Federation in the three months since I was notified about my membership application. But that was all about to change.

An email from the General Secretary appeared in my inbox. It was one of those group emails that I hate with a passion. Some people think these emails are a great idea because it saves them writing to all their friends individually. I disagree. To me, it's like they're saying, 'You're special, but not that special.' At least make me feel important by cutting and pasting the same message and starting it with 'Dear Mick'.

The email was sent to all the members of the WPF, asking if we would be sending a national team to India for the World Sudoku Championship. I hadn't done anything about it, so replied that Australia would not be sending a team. I thought that would be the end of it.

I don't know when some people sleep. And I don't know how they can work such long hours and still function. If I do one twelve-hour day I'm exhausted. Let alone doing back-to-back ones and clocking up a sixty-hour week. I need to work, relax and then sleep.

It was 6.28pm that same day and I was on the couch at home. Mucking around on my laptop, I decided to check my emails. There was one from Hendrik Hardeman, the organiser of the World Sudoku Championship in Goa, India. I clicked on it. One thousand and seventy-two words later, I was feeling extremely stressed. I was being put under immense pressure to get a team to India.

He started his email by telling me he was surprised to learn the WPF board had granted me membership. In his opinion, there were other puzzle publishers who would have been a more obvious choice. He made it clear I had to get actively involved and stated that if he had to do all the work on his own, there was no reason for him to protect or promote my interests.

He was bowling short ball after short ball, each rearing up towards my throat. It was intimidating stuff and it kept on coming.

He wanted me to approach Qantas and see if they had a special fare for Australian team members, approach potential sponsors about helping to cover the costs, talk to newspapers about promoting the event and organise something online.

He finished his first email reinforcing how important it was to have a team from Australia in Goa, and how they'd appreciate it very much if I took responsibility for this as the official WPF member.

With beads of sweat forming on my brow, I sent a nervous reply and came clean. I told him I'd originally planned to run my own World Sudoku Championship and the main reason I joined the WPF was because I wanted to represent Australia. I explained how I didn't belong to a full-time puzzle company, how I agreed there were probably better candidates, and how I was only given membership because no one else put their hand up. I finished by apologising for not having done more and said I'd do what I could to help.

At 9.43pm, he'd sent me another one. Apparently, my response convinced him that I was motivated enough and we should try to make it work together.

Great.

The next day, Hendrik sent me another six emails, the last at 10.22pm. He stressed that if there was anything I needed, all I had to do was ask. He was working fourteen-hour days, seven days a week. I had no escape and no excuse.

If I thought that would be it for a while, I was sadly mistaken. My next email arrived at 3.47am. He wasn't kidding when he said he was working long hours. This one scared me. He sent, in detail, notes on how to run state and national championships. I was overwhelmed by his expectations.

He wanted me to get an article about the World Sudoku Championships published in all the national newspapers and then another article to promote the start dates of the Australian tournament. There would be a qualifying round, with puzzles appearing in the paper and also on the Australian championships website, which I was supposed to design and build.

When the tournament proper started, people would have two days to submit their answers to four separate puzzles. To submit an answer, the puzzlers would extract four special digits from each solved puzzle to form a six-digit code. These six-digit codes would be submitted online, via SMS or by phone to a call centre.

Each correct puzzle would score a certain number of points and the time that each answer was submitted would also be recorded to decide winners in the event of a tie. Once the rankings were done, I'd invite the top forty or fifty to participate in a written test the following week. I'd simply have to find a hotel or other venue prepared to provide the space. For the written test, Hendrik suggested I use between six and eight puzzles. When someone completed all the puzzles, they would raise their hand and a volunteer would collect their booklet, note the time taken to complete the puzzles and hand it to the marker. The first person to solve all the puzzles would be declared the winner.

Where Hendrik saw solutions, all I saw was a lot of work. Work I really did not want to do. SMS platforms, websites, call centres, volunteers, venues. I wouldn't have known where to start even if I had felt keen. The worst thing was, if the guilt got to me and I somehow managed to organise everything, I wouldn't even get to play for Australia because there was no way in the world I would win. I still hadn't even attempted a puzzle, let alone completed one faster than everyone else in Australia. The whole exercise defeated the purpose. I was supposed to spend hours and hours of my time running an event I had no interest in for the benefit of everyone except myself.

I wanted out.

My bluff had been called and I was in way over my head. I sent an email to Hendrik, saying I just didn't have the time to organise anything and suggested that he contact a puzzle publisher to see if they could help. I was exhausted at the mere thought of being involved and it felt like a weight had been lifted off my shoulders when I finally announced I was pulling out.

To his credit, Hendrik was great about it. He said he'd

approach a specialist puzzle company with more resources at its disposal and keep me up to date with how things progressed. The relief I felt was enormous.

When I was sharing a house with some mates in Shenton Park in Perth during the early nineties, a pigeon walked in through our front door. It must either have been someone's pet or unbelievably stupid because it had no fear. It would come in, walk around the living room, dodge flying rugby balls, jump up on the table, peck around, then wander back to wherever it had come from. It had no problem with us picking it up and putting it outside if we had to leave the house before it did. It was bizarre because we did nothing to encourage it to stay. But it did. We simply couldn't get rid of it.

A bit like Hendrik.

In an email titled 'More bad news', Hendrik told me the other puzzle company he had asked to help organise the Australian team had also pulled out. He was desperate to get an Australian team to India, had spent countless hours trying to get me to help and had been knocked back by the people he felt should have been the WPF member in the first place.

I'm obviously a sucker. I felt bad for the poor bloke because he'd busted a gut trying to get something happening in Australia and all his work had amounted to zero. I let my heart rule my head and, without thinking, said I could possibly hold a very small competition in Western Australia and call it the Australian Championship. If people from the east kicked up a stink because they didn't know about it, we'd tell them we'd put them on the mailing list for the following year.

He liked what he was hearing. And then he sent a reply that was like a 'get out of jail free' card. He said he wasn't concerned how I selected an Australian team and to do whatever I could in WA to get a team to Goa.

In my mind, that meant I could stick a few posters on telegraph poles and maybe tape a piece of paper to the window of the local IGA as a way of advertising the Australian Sudoku Championship. Basically, if someone turned up, they could play. And if they wanted to go to India, they could help themselves. If no one turned up, I'd lie. I'd tell Hendrik we had heaps of people but, unfortunately, no one was prepared to fork out their hard-earned to pay for the trip overseas.

I'd have done my bit for the WPF and Hendrik would be satisfied that his efforts hadn't been in vain. Everyone would be happy. Especially me.

CHAPTER 9
Regrets

It's funny how some things seem like a good idea at the time.

There's a race in NSW called the Hawkesbury Canoe Classic. It's a 111-kilometre flat-water paddle along the Hawkesbury River, from Windsor in Sydney's west to Brooklyn, a sleepy inlet town about an hour north of Sydney.

The event attracts about 600 craft and begins at 6pm. The theory is that you get to paddle through the sunset, along a glassy river in the light of the full moon and continue through sunrise the following morning. There are various checkpoints along the way where you can pull in and meet up with your support crew, who provide much needed nourishment and encouragement before sending you on your way again.

A mate and I decided we should enter on a double ski. We were paddling in the occasional surf carnival for Bilgola, a club on Sydney's spectacular northern beaches, and thought the event would be a bit of fun. Or at least a bit different.

As part of our preparation, we did a fair bit of training on the Lane Cove River and down around The Spit at Mosman. The scenery was stunning and it was a great way to get a different perspective on the hidden treasures that abound in one of the world's most beautiful cities.

The training sessions served two purposes. First, they helped our fitness in areas we didn't expect, like our bums and wrists. We were never going to paddle at a speed where our heart rates would be overly high, so it was more a case of getting used to sitting on the ski for long hours and getting our shoulders and arms accustomed to the endless repetition.

It was also a great chance to work out how we could best fit-out our craft so we could survive the distances between checkpoints. It was a marathon paddle, so we needed to carry a certain amount of food and drink with us.

I don't care how well you know someone. When you're with them for more than a few hours, you're going to run out of things to say. Especially when the only thing you're seeing is the back of the person in front of you. We knew we'd need some sort of stimulation during the paddle and decided music would be the answer.

The ipod and Mp3 players were yet to be invented. The Walkman was considered cutting edge. My mate and I still needed to communicate, so wearing headphones wasn't really an option. We decided to create our own on-board stereo system.

We started with an old chlorine bucket, which was white, plastic and about forty centimetres tall. We cut two slits, three centimetres long, on opposite sides at the base and then threaded strapping tape through the holes, underneath the ski and back up again. We did this a few times to make sure the bucket was firmly attached to the deck.

From there, we taped a plastic bag to the top edge of the bucket, to give us a makeshift waterproof lining that would keep everything dry. On the lid, we strapped an old car stereo speaker – the type that comes in a black plastic mount and normally sits on the flat area behind the back seat. A small hole provided a safe passage for the speaker wire, which was attached to a jack that fit the hole for headphones in a small tape deck. We put the tape deck in the plastic bag, plugged in the speaker, then put the lid on the bucket.

It looked ridiculous, but it worked. Our stereo resembled a chimney stack on a barge. We had sacrificed aerodynamics for practicality but had plenty of room for all the refreshments we'd need. We could paddle for weeks.

Our first training run with our new contraption was fantastic. We had a truckload of cassettes and spent our session paddling and singing along to Mental as Anything, Skyhooks and The Little River Band. We were ready to race.

Stew Jenkins headed our support crew. He's a nuggety, good-humoured bloke, who's up for pretty much anything. Which was just as well. He drove a Kombi van decked out with cooking facilities and a bed, which was ideal, given that he'd be spending long periods of time waiting for us to arrive at the various checkpoints.

The first of these was about sixteen kilometres in, but Stew and his team missed it. That wasn't as bad as it sounds and not completely unexpected. It was less than two hours into the race so we were still feeling pretty comfortable.

Night was fast approaching. We had a couple of Milk Arrowroot biscuits and a stretch before igniting the green cyalume sticks tied to our ski and paddling on. We didn't meet up with Stewie until the 40-kilometre checkpoint. That was the furthest we had ever paddled in one go and we were starting to feel it. The worst part was we still had seventy-one kilometres left. We were tired and sore, and my paddling partner was vomiting. It was going to be a long night.

After a drink and a bite to eat, we farewelled our crew, who told us they were going to miss the next couple of checkpoints so they could get a bit further down river, set up and have a couple of beers. I was glad they were enjoying themselves.

Back on the water and in a world of hurt, but with the vomiting over, we decided to crank up the stereo. I put in our 'Best of the Deltones' cassette and pressed play. It's amazing how much difference a bit of music can make. It was the middle of the night, pitch black and all of a sudden we were having a ball.

When we started playing the music we were on our own. By about the third song, we were the main attraction. One green glow stick after another started coming towards us, like mutant radioactive moths to a flame. It seemed everyone needed a boost and our stereo system was the perfect remedy. Different paddlers would sit with us for a while, recharge their mental batteries and then slowly pull away, the dulcet sounds of the Deltones still ringing in their ears.

One thing we were supposed to do at the first checkpoint was get some more cassettes. We probably should have written it down somewhere, because we completely forgot. It's not that we didn't like the Deltones. Far from it. But when it's the only music you have, it starts to get on your nerves a bit the fifth time it's played.

The novelty of the music also wore off for the other paddlers and we were soon on our own again, battling fatigue. There were no green dots visible in front or behind. Despite having someone else on the ski with me, I felt very lonely. The rhythmical sound of our blades hitting the water was almost hypnotic.

When it's dark and you're tired, your mind starts to play tricks and it becomes hard to navigate. If there are gaps in the trees along the river bank, it looks like that's where the river goes. When the ski comes to a sudden stop, you realise it's not. So you paddle backwards, back into the middle of the river, and keep going.

Then repeat.

No one said this race would be easy.

Also, the Hawkesbury is tidal and paddling against it when you have nothing left in the tank is soul destroying. The initial enthusiasm I had for the event was but a distant memory.

You'd think crossing the finish line after fifteen gruelling hours of paddling would be cause for celebration. It wasn't. We'd all had a gutful. We put the ski on the roof, got in the Kombi and left. We hardly even spoke, we were so tired. I was asleep by the time we got out of the car park. Poor old Stew still had an hour and a half of driving ahead of him. The thankless task of the support crew.

The next year, my good mate Marty Roebuck thought he'd like to try it. He teamed up with Scott Johnson, the first grade captain at Eastwood and a man who would go on to coach the Wallabies backs for the 2007 Rugby World Cup and then the American Eagles rugby team.

There's a theory called 'specificity of training', which means if you're a runner, you run. If you're a swimmer, you swim. If your event involves short sprints, you do short sprints. It makes perfect sense. Marty and Scott were about to paddle 111 kilometres. They played rugby.

The record time for a double ski is eight hours eighteen minutes. One of the paddlers in that team was Brett Worth, who studied phys ed in the year above me at college. Scott Johnson was in the year below me. Matt Diegutis was in my year and he holds the record for the single kayak in the over-40s class. He did the race in eight hours thirty minutes. Matt's time as a veteran is only forty-one seconds outside the open record for the single kayak. So Scott, at least, had good paddling pedigree, even if it was by default.

Marty had two aims for the race.
1. To finish.
2. To beat my time.

One out of two isn't bad. He finished in seventeen hours forty-one minutes, two hours slower than I did, and to this day will tell anyone who'll listen that it was the toughest thing he's ever done.

When he was in the middle of his decorated Wallaby career, he was often asked to fill out profiles in rugby magazines. One of the more common questions was to name his toughest opponent. It was never the All Blacks, South Africa or one of the other major rugby nations. He always wrote the Hawkesbury Classic.

Telling Hendrik I'd organise a scaled-down version of an Australian Sudoku Championship was another thing that seemed like a good idea at the time. But, once again, the more I thought about it, the more I regretted having made the offer.

I ran the scenarios through my head.

What would happen if I stuck a sign up somewhere and ten people saw it and thought, 'That sounds like fun'? What if they told five people each and then those people told five people each? Suddenly, that one sign would have resulted in 250 people expecting to compete. I'd need to find a hall. Then I'd need enough tables and chairs. Then I'd need puzzles. Then I'd need to put those puzzles in a booklet. Then I'd need people to help me set up the hall and hand out the booklets. Then I'd need someone to look after the timing, someone to collect the completed puzzle books and someone to mark them all.

I'm not passionate about sudoku. I knew that if I were, I could probably have pulled it off. But I wasn't. What I had thought would be easy was turning out to be the exact opposite.

So I decided against organising a scaled-down Australian Sudoku Championship and went to plan B.

I recalled Hendrik's email in which he said he wasn't concerned about how I selected an Australian team and to do whatever I could in WA to get a team to Goa.

I didn't want to go to India and I couldn't afford to even if I had wanted to. But I had the power to choose an Australian team. I didn't think the WPF would renew my membership, so this was my one and only chance to use my role. I knew I wasn't the only person who dreamed of representing their country, so I wanted to give someone with the desire, the time and the money, the opportunity.

I drafted a letter explaining how I ended up as the sole selector for the Australian Sudoku Team. I explained that competing at the World Sudoku Championship was a once-in-a-lifetime opportunity to officially wear the green and gold. I explained that it was an honour that no one could ever take away from you. How it was one of those stories you'd tell your grandchildren about.

The more I wrote, the more I wished I was going. It sounded amazing. I was envious of the people who would take up the offer and I knew I'd regret not taking it up myself.

I guess it just wasn't meant to be.

CHAPTER 10

I'm In

Sandy Sutherland is a unique individual. He has an IQ of 160, which puts him in the genius class. It's an amazing score. Amazing because, to meet him, you wouldn't think it was possible. Sandy is living proof you can play contact sport without a helmet and enjoy a regular beverage or three and still have a brilliant mind.

He has an executive-level job with an international company that takes him around the world. He has every right to be your typical corporate wanker. The type who only eats at five-star restaurants and swirls his glass of red before sniffing it and making some observation about the bouquet. But he's nothing like that. Not even close.

Sandy has remained more grounded than an emu. And it's why he's such a well-liked bloke. He's a great character and extremely loyal to his mates. He'd be living somewhere in Europe and hear about a birthday, barbecue or other special event in Perth. He'd fly in especially for it then leave, hungover, the next day to resume his responsibilities at work, even though he hadn't slept for the best part of three days.

We played rugby together for University. He was a tough competitor who would constantly get smashed but always get up. He wasn't blessed with speed or size but he never held back.

His playing weight was around seventy-five kilograms and the representative selectors always said he was too light. They said he needed to be around ninety kilograms. He hit ninety-five kilograms a couple of years ago and wants to know where all those selectors are now.

One was about to come looking for him.

I was going to send the letter I'd drafted about playing for Australia at the World Sudoku Championship to the secretary of our rugby club and ask for it to be circulated to all the members. I figured if I couldn't go, I would at least have a connection to someone who did. I'd ridden on coat-tails before; there was no reason to stop now.

Then I remembered Sandy.

He was the sort of guy who would like this sort of thing. See the funny side of it. He was always up for an adventure and a laugh, so I decided to send it to him first.

I sent the email at 10.44am Perth time:

Hey Sandy
 I'm about to release the attached to the rugby club but thought I'd run it past you first.
 If you're keen, let me know.

Sandy was living in Switzerland. I don't know what the time difference was. But at 9.24pm Perth time, I received his response:

I'm in.
 I have never played sudoku — but I am sure I can work it out on the day.

Before I had time to acknowledge his email, another appeared:

> *Actually — let me clarify that — I am in if you mean that yourself, myself, Hamish and Skiffo are heading over.*
> *Absolutely no interest otherwise.*

I don't know how long I stared at that email. I just know it had a huge effect on me. Suddenly, everything changed. Everything became clear. It took the whole thing to a new level.

Before, I had felt like it would have just been me heading to India. Possibly with people I knew but probably with people I wouldn't normally choose to go with. Now, I was looking at achieving my dream with three mates. Mates I had known and played rugby with for many years. We all would have loved to have played for Australia together. Now we had the chance. Sandy was keen, but only if it was with his brother Hamish, Skiffo and me. The same Skiffo who had sat with me on that plane to Brisbane just eight months earlier. The same Skiffo who had introduced me to the game that set the whole process in motion.

It must have been fate. Sandy could have said he wasn't interested or that he'd think about it. But he was crystal clear. He was in.

For some reason, I had never considered simply inviting three mates to join me in the team. Now it was the most obvious thing in the world to do.

India? I'd always wanted to go to India. And I'd heard Goa was beautiful at that time of year.

CHAPTER 11

Opportunities

Growing up, there were two things I was scared of. One was failure. The other was sharks.

Unfortunately, I've crossed paths with failure more times than I care to remember and it doesn't have the same hold on me as it used to. As the ancient Greek storyteller Aesop famously said, 'Familiarity breeds contempt.'

Sharks, on the other hand, still scare the shit out of me.

I was a member of North Cottesloe Surf Club for a number of years, an organisation with the unenviable title of 'host club' for the two most recent shark attacks in metropolitan Perth.

I used to do weights in the club's gym every Tuesday and Thursday morning. If there was a decent swell running, I'd forget the weights, grab my ski and paddle down to a reef break called Deep Six and catch some waves for an hour.

One morning, I got to the gym and noticed there was a bit of a wave on. It was overcast and there was a slight onshore breeze, so the surface of the water was a bit bumpy. I didn't really feel like doing weights but I was getting fussy in my old age and didn't feel like paddling in those less-than-perfect conditions either. So I stayed put.

Not long before I arrived at the gym, club member Brian Sierakowski, a lawyer and former St Kilda footballer, had taken a double ski with Barney Hanrahan and headed down towards Deep Six.

As I was lying on the mat trying to motivate myself to do something, two more members, namely Malcolm McCusker and his wife Di, walked in. Malcolm was about to head off on his normal morning paddle when Di said she might join him. So instead of taking his single ski, Malcolm grabbed another double.

A few hours later I was at work when Skiffo rang and told me Brian had been attacked by a shark. As it turned out, a five-metre white pointer had used the double ski like it was a toothpick. The shark bit the ski in two, just a few centimetres in front of Brian's feet. As he and Barney tried to keep their balance, the shark kept chewing. Both men were thrown into the water. As they fell, Brian was hit in the face by the shark's tail.

As the shark turned around, Malcolm and Di arrived at the same spot. With no regard for their own safety, they paddled in, picked up Brian and Barney and rushed them back to the shore.

I saw what was left of the ski a few weeks later. If the shark had attacked any further down the ski, Brian would have lost both feet at best. If Di hadn't wanted to paddle that morning, Malcolm would have been on the smaller, single ski. Would he have been able to get Brian and Barney on that ski and get them to safety? If I had decided to paddle that morning, would I have been the target? If I had been an observer, would I have reacted as quickly as Malcolm and Di had? We'll never know. Thankfully, luck was on everyone's side.

Three years later, a second shark attack disturbed the usual tranquillity of a late spring morning at North Cottesloe. As patrons enjoyed their coffee and breakfast at the Blue Duck Café overlooking the beach, Ken Crew finished a relaxing swim with a group of friends. Suddenly, as the café goers watched in horror, a five-metre white pointer shark ploughed into the swimmers. Ken bore the brunt of the attack and, sadly, passed away on the beach from a loss of blood, despite the frantic efforts of his rescuers.

It was unbelievable. Things like that just don't happen at one of Perth's most famous beaches. The tragic incident shook the entire community. As the enormity of what had happened sunk in, people started thinking about how it could have been them. No one felt safe anymore and people stopped swimming there. I know, because I was one of them. Even now, I can't swim more than about twenty-five metres off the beach without getting spooked.

What happened to Brian and Ken makes you realise that you can't take life for granted. You really need to make the most of the opportunities presented to you.

It was going to cost me around $3500 to go to India. Not to travel and experience the culture, but for sudoku, a game I'd never played before. That was a lot of money. And there were far better uses for it. We needed a new back fence, for a start. The car had an oil leak that needed to be fixed. There were school fees to pay.

But I knew it would be great fun, especially with Hamish, Sandy and Skiffo. I remember running it by Sharan. I didn't know what her reaction would be but, to her credit, she was supportive. She thought the whole thing was completely bizarre but that if I was that desperate to play for Australia, I should go for it. Especially given the quality of my team mates. As she said, the trip to India was something I really wanted to do. I should take the opportunity while I could. The fence and the oil leak could wait.

No wonder I married her.

CHAPTER 12

Picked

I was going on a tour to India to represent my country.

The more I said it, the better it sounded. And the more I said it, the more excited I became.

It was surreal. I couldn't believe I was on the verge of achieving my dream. I also couldn't believe I had almost let the chance go by. What was I thinking?

So many positives came out of Sandy's email. Even for my two boys. They could already say their mum played for Australia. In a few months' time, they would be able to say their dad did too.

It's amazing how your enthusiasm levels rise when you know you'll be a direct beneficiary of your efforts.

For the sake of posterity, I decided to hold the first-ever Australian Sudoku Championship, and emailed the details to Sandy, Hamish and Skiffo. It was to be held at the Ocean Beach Hotel in Cottesloe, the scene of many memorable evenings. It was like our home ground.

When the big day arrived, there was a definite buzz of excitement. The sun was shining, birds were singing. It was a perfect Sunday afternoon. Around 120 people were there but only four of us knew that history was about to take place.

We had a few beers and a bowl of chips to calm the nerves. Slowly, the tension started to build. Then, without so much as looking at a puzzle, we called for the envelope.

I don't know why I was so nervous. I was the sole selector after all. And I'd already picked the team.

Then, at precisely 4.27pm, the first-ever Australian sudoku team was announced:

> *Ladies and gentlemen. It gives me great pleasure to announce that Mick Colliss, Mark Skiffington, Hamish Sutherland and Sandy Sutherland have been chosen to represent Australia at the World Sudoku Championship in Goa, India.*

I've often wondered what it must be like to hear your name called out as a member of an Australian team. I thought back to Ian Williams and the day we were delivering phone books. I thought about Marty Roebuck. I thought about Sharan.

It was the fulfilment of a lifetime's ambition. The proudest moment of our lives, to sit there and think we'd done it. We'd joined the ranks of the privileged few. We'd been chosen to represent Australia.

We celebrated with a few more beers and hot chips. But we still had one more thing to announce.

No Australian team is complete without a captain. And there is no greater honour than being chosen as the person to lead your nation's representatives.

Skiffo and I first met in 1988, when I arrived in Perth. We played a season of rugby and studied together before I headed back to Sydney the following year. Skiffo won a scholarship to play rugby in Scotland and when I returned to Perth for the start of the season in 1990, he was still away.

When he got back, he had nowhere to live. I didn't know him all that well but we got on, so I offered him a space in my living room. It wasn't much but it was somewhere he could put a bed and he was welcome to stay for as long as he wanted.

We ended up sharing a variety of different places for the next seven years. He's a great mate. One of the best. He'd do anything for you, without question.

Skiffo was the one who let me stay on the floor in his room when a large rat moved into mine.

He was the one who put his hand up to go into the ceiling to put down some bait when everyone else was too scared to. We'd seen those rats and they were huge. His only condition was that he had to wear a pair of swimming goggles during the exercise because his dear mother had warned him early to beware of rats because 'they'll go for your eyes'.

But perhaps his greatest display of selflessness came about when I had my car stolen. It was the middle of the surf club season, and because I was paddling my ski nearly every day, I used to just leave it and a mate's ski on the roof of my HQ Kingswood wagon in between sessions. One morning, I got up to go training and discovered my car was gone. The car was worth about $1000. The two skis on the roof were worth about $2500. I rang my training partner and told him I couldn't paddle that morning. Then I proceeded to tell him that he couldn't either because his ski, my ski and my car had all been stolen.

There was little I could do about it but I didn't want to do nothing so I rang a terrific bloke by the name of Charles Forbes, the father of a friend from university. He agreed to drive around with me on the off chance we might find the car dumped somewhere. It never had much petrol so chances were good it wouldn't be too far away.

I spent the best part of the morning on a fruitless search through various suburbs. When I returned home about four hours later, I couldn't believe my eyes. My car – complete with the skis unharmed and still strapped to the roof – was parked outside our house.

In the time I'd been out searching, the police had rung to say they'd found it abandoned in some bush, and Skiffo went out to pick it up and drive it home.

While it's a nice gesture on Skiffo's part, it's not something out of the ordinary. Any mate would do it. The thing that made it special was the fact that the thieves had done a poo in the back. I understand that when you've gotta go, you've gotta go. But surely they could have done their business outside the car. Even if, for some amazing reason, they did have to poo inside the car, did they really have to then go and smear it all over the back windows?

No one else would go anywhere near it. Not the people who found it, not the police, not the tow-truck driver. The only one who would was Skiffo.

He drove that car back to our place, like the man from Snowy River bringing in the colt from old Regret. He had his head out the window the entire way, dry-retching and gagging at the stench as the sun slowly baked the moist, brown clumps into a solid crust behind him.

And so, years after this, it was with tears of pride and a lump in my throat that I announced to all at the Ocean Beach Hotel on that sunny Sunday afternoon that the first captain of the Australian Sudoku Team was none other than Mark Anthony Skiffington. My mate.

While it was a position of privilege, Mark had virtually chosen himself. He was the only one of the newly formed Australian team who had actually completed a puzzle. He would join the likes of Mark Taylor, Steve Waugh, Adam Gilchrist and the greats before them, as one of the rare individuals selected to lead an Australian team to India.

I picked myself as the Australian vice-captain, then set about the task of choosing something equally important: the team uniform. None of us would ever get to wear the green and gold again, so we had to make sure we had enough gear to last us well into the next decade.

We devised a wish list and set about filling it. Letters were written and calls made to Adidas, Nike and Reebok. I made contact with the people at Rossi Boots. To a man, they declined the offer to support the Australian Sudoku Team.

I've always been a big fan of FILA sports gear. Now I think I'd like to be buried in it. FILA came to the party in a big way and I can't thank them enough. Our timing was good because they were having an end-of-season sale, where most of the gear was fifty per cent off anyway. Head office threw in an extra ten per cent and wished us well at the tournament. It was great to see a big company get behind the underdog.

I also took Hendrik's advice and filled out a sponsorship request form for Qantas. I didn't demand free flights; I just said if there was anything Australia's national airline could do to help Australia's first-ever national sudoku team, it would be much appreciated.

I'm still waiting to hear back.

It was a shame we were going to India and not somewhere cold, like Iceland. We were all very keen to get tracksuits and hoodies embroidered with the coat of arms on the breast and AUSTRALIA emblazoned across our shoulders. But we knew we wouldn't get any use out of them on the tour, so went for the summer selection instead.

Walking into the FILA store to dress the team was very exciting. We didn't have a set budget but I figured if we were getting things at half price, I could buy twenty-five per cent more gear than I needed and still come out in front.

So I did.

The next item on the agenda was the embroidery. We found a beautiful coat of arms and had a special template made up that contained the words 'Australian Sudoku Team, World Championship, India 2008'. We embroidered both on everything.

No touring uniform would be complete without the Number 1s – the formal gear. I couldn't believe it when I stumbled across a company in the United States that would customise a tie with sudoku puzzles and the word Australia printed on the front. I ordered four straight away.

Our blazers were a direct replica of the ones worn by the 1936 Australian Olympic team – bottle green with gold trim around the wrists and at the top of the pockets. The material was bought locally and shipped to Bali. If you're going to make a replica, you may as well get it done by the professionals.

The only thing left was our playing kit. We wanted something green and gold that would be comfortable. The playing conditions would be tough, so we needed something light and airy. Something that wouldn't retain our body odours. Again by chance, I discovered a wholesaler in Sydney who had exactly what we needed.

I tried every piece of kit on when I got it home from the embroiderer's. Every piece except my Australian playing uniform. I was saving that precious moment for the dressing room in India.

When we finally packed our bags, our kit was as good as any representative side I had ever been involved with:

1 x blazer
1 x long grey pants
1 x sudoku tie
2 x polo shirts
1 x T-shirt
1 x singlet
1 x walk shorts
1 x sports shorts
1 x board shorts
1 x stubby holder
2 x caps (one with bottle opener in the peak)
1 x green and gold playing shirt
1 x green and gold playing shorts
1 x pair green and gold thongs.

When I was a young kid running around in the Under 8s for St Michael's at Meadowbank, my father always made sure everyone had matching shorts, socks and jerseys. He said to me, 'If you can't play like a team, you can at least look like one.'

I think he would have been very proud.

CHAPTER 13

Mates

There are some great nicknames in world sport. William Perry, the 174-kilogram former defensive lineman for the Chicago Bears, was known as 'The Refrigerator'. Jerry Collins, the fearsome ex-All Blacks flanker, was known as 'The Terminator'. Trevor Gillmeister, the Brisbane Broncos and Australian rugby league hard man, was known as 'The Axe'.

I was known as 'The Blancmange'. The dictionary reveals it to be a soft, custard-like dessert. Not exactly flattering, but my style of play meant I was never going to have a moniker like 'Cement'.

I was pretty good at avoiding the physical contests that play such a big role in a collision sport like rugby. Some people relish that part of the game but it wasn't really my cup of tea. I loved being part of the team though, and thankfully my contribution was enough to keep me in the side.

As much as I enjoyed playing, I loved what happened after the final whistle the most. I loved the emotion – the happiness or disappointment. Sport tends to amplify emotions. Watch any sport, especially at the elite level, and you'll understand what I mean. In a tight game, sensible men and women will jump from their seats and scream without even thinking about it. If their team loses, it's not unusual to see them more upset than the players are. I remember crying when Nick Whitford kicked a penalty goal in the last minute to win our Under 15s grand final. I just couldn't help it. I wasn't generally the emotional type but that game of rugby reduced me to tears. Not much else has.

Even my wedding didn't. I had a great day and I loved watching Sharan walk down the aisle. But when the priest said, 'I now pronounce you husband and wife', I didn't start jumping up and down, cheering and punching the air. Not like I did when Stirling Mortlock took that intercept against the All Blacks in the semifinal of the 2003 Rugby World Cup.

I loved sitting in the dressing room after the game, having a cold beer. I loved feeling sore and fatigued. I loved the camaraderie. Being part of the inner circle of guys who were actually out there in the middle, not just a spectator. I can understand those people who find it hard to watch sport when they've retired.

There's something very special about playing sport with your mates. It's the only reason I ever played. I didn't need it to keep fit or as a legitimate excuse to get some peace away from the wife and kids for a few precious hours every week. It was purely because of the guys I played alongside.

It would be the same with sudoku.

We gave Sandy the nickname 'Rain Man' after the character played by Dustin Hoffman in the film of the same name. Dustin's character didn't come across as all that bright but he was brilliant when it came to numbers. Sandy hadn't played sudoku before but he was extremely intelligent; Skiffo thinks he's borderline autistic. Sandy was the dark horse. Our game breaker. The super-sub we'd rely on to make a real impact when it was needed most.

Sandy's brother, Hamish, has always been known as 'Hamo'. A phys ed teacher by trade, he was the elder statesman of the team but looked younger than all of us. He is one of the most naturally gifted athletes I have ever met, with a physique that made the rest of us look obese. The World Sudoku Championship would be his second taste of international competition, having played for Western Australia against the All Blacks in 1988.

Hamish and Sandy have one of the closest relationships I've ever seen between two brothers. If my two boys have anything similar, I'll feel I've succeeded as a parent. When they'd turn up to play rugby they reminded me of the Blues Brothers. A big, old, white Holden station wagon would rattle in, the doors would creak open, empty beer cans would spill out, followed closely by Hamish, Sandy and their two dogs, Leroy and Wazza. Nothing fazed the Sutherland brothers. No opponent intimidated them and every situation had a funny side.

If I had a nickname away from the world of rugby, it would be Jack. Simply because I'm the quintessential jack of all trades, master of none. I've tried most things – sports commentary, writing poetry and doing emcee work. I've won a couple of awards for advertising, played rugby for WA, raced in triathlons and been a very ordinary iron man. Compared with the average punter, I was okay. But I never excelled in any of these things. I can now add vice-captain of the Australian Sudoku Team to my list of achievements. The nickname won't be changing any time soon, I'm sure.

Skiffo is known by many names. Skivvy, Skip, Bubba, Big Fella. But Skiffo is the most common. He's a solid, heavily muscled unit who also played rugby for Western Australia against international teams. He has a massive arse and, if someone had only noticed it, I think he would have made a great sprint cyclist. Come to think of it, I'm not sure how anyone missed it. He's a stockbroker by trade but now lists his occupation as captain of the Australian Sudoku Team.

Mateship is a huge part of Australia's national psyche. It's up there with the ANZAC spirit, the bronzed Aussie and the larrikin. For me, there's nothing like it. Growing up, none of my mates had girlfriends – we had each other. We'd spend our time up at the park kicking a footy. Or, when it was raining, we'd be diving and sliding on the wet grass as we practised scoring tries.

I think I liked having mates more than having a girlfriend because mates never put you under pressure or have unrealistic expectations. They take you as you are, no questions asked.

I should have bought a house years ago. I'd be hundreds of thousands of dollars better off. But it didn't even cross my mind. I was too busy renting other people's houses with my mates.

For about four years, there were five of us living in a place in Claremont, one of Perth's more affluent suburbs. We were paying $50 a week each. I remember one summer, we all bought a pair of pyjamas in our favourite rugby league team's colours. We took them to the local markets and had our favourite players' names printed across the shoulders and their numbers on our backs. We wore them every night.

Once, during a commercial break on TV, Skiffo and I did a chocolate run down to the chemist at the end of our street. The girl serving behind the counter looked at us in a peculiar way and said, 'You're in your pyjamas.' We answered matter-of-factly, 'Well, it is past eight o'clock.'

I think this whole 'find a girl and settle down' mentality is overrated. And, come to think of it, I reckon we shouldn't be so quick to dismiss polygamy either. What's wrong with having one wife to cook for you, another to clean for you, another really good-looking one to sleep with you and a bunch of mates to play with you, all living happily together in the same house?

I love it when I see blokes doing the weekly shopping together. A packet of Coco Pops, Tim Tams, milk, bread, ice-cream and a few bananas. It's a simple, stress-free existence.

I used to love sitting around watching shows like 'Baywatch' with my mates. Seeing how many times we could bounce a ball off a wall and catch it in our non-dominant hand. Having conversations about nothing, long before Seinfeld made a career out of it. I used to love riding three abreast on the bench seat of the Kingswood. It was never two in the front, one in the back.

I'm jealous now when I see guys living like that. I'd never give up what I have, but I love getting back to basics. Just me and my mates.

That's what going to India as part of an Australian team was all about.

Chapter 14

Lights, camera, action

Underwhelmed would be an understatement.

After all the grief Hendrik gave me about living up to expectations and fulfilling my role as the member of the WPF, he didn't even reply when I sent him an excited email with the news that I'd managed to organise an Australian Championship and would be sending a team to India.

I didn't expect him to jump for joy. I just wanted him to acknowledge my email. But I got nothing.

Little wonder, really. I had panicked at the thought of running a local championship. He was trying to organise a World Championship. I guess he had other things on his mind.

When we first thought about wearing the green and gold, it was a personal thing. But I soon realised we weren't just doing it for ourselves. What we had achieved, and how we achieved it, struck a chord with the Australian public. Word quickly started to spread and the number of well-wishers started to grow.

Average Australians thought our story was great. A group of mates who had always dreamed about representing their country finally get their chance – playing sudoku. A game most of them can't even play.

Ryan Rampling, the highly talented producer of the 6PR breakfast show in Perth, offered to be our media manager. I didn't know what he thought he could do, but he's a terrific bloke and I was happy for him to run with it.

And run with it he did.

The Australian Sudoku Team had its first public airing on the show Ryan produced. I wore my Number 1s into the station and was interviewed about my lack of sudoku ability and about the forthcoming World Championship. I was also asked if I felt bad that I would be representing Australia when there were people far better than I was at the game who would be missing out.

My reply was simple. No.

I didn't feel bad at all. It wasn't my fault Australia's elite sudoku players didn't know about the World Sudoku Championship and it wasn't my fault none of the puzzling companies had bothered to tell them. I thought if I could help spread the word, Australia would be in a position to send a stronger team the following year.

I knew our team wouldn't exactly set the sudoku world on fire, but Australia had to start somewhere. The first year the Canterbury Crusaders played in the Super 12 rugby competition, they finished last. Three years later, they won and went on to become the dominant team in the competition. We wanted to establish a presence and build a platform for the future.

The only thing missing was a name.

Australia has the Wallabies, the Kangaroos, the Socceroos and the Hockeyroos. 6PR's breakfast team of Steve Mills and Tony McManus challenged the people of Perth to come up with a suitable nickname for us. As the Australian member of the WPF, I could decide there and then, so the listeners knew they'd have a result by the end of the show.

We were inundated with calls and ended up with a shortlist of four: The Echidnas, because we were funny pricks; The Camels, because India was a long way to go for a drink; and, The Sudokuroos.

I thought The Camels was the most accurate, but we were conscious of giving the team a name for eternity, not just a one-off. Hopefully, the next Australian team would give the competition a real shake.

In the end, we chose the remaining option, The Numbats. It's an Australian marsupial with strong links to Western Australia, so the Australian sudoku team's heritage would always be remembered. It was also a word similar to 'numbers', so it was perfect. In addition, the numbat only mates once a year. We connected on so many levels.

6PR has a varied listening audience. When we announced the name, Paul Kelly, a great supporter of the station, and the National Advertising and Sponsorship Manager of Members Equity Bank, sent a text message to Tony. He said he liked the story and thought 'The Members Equity Numbats' had a nice ring to it.

So did I.

As soon as my interview was over, I tracked down Paul's number and gave him a call. He obviously has a similar sense of humour to the team because he asked me to put a proposal together and said that, if it was acceptable, he'd consider providing financial support in exchange for the naming rights. What a champion bloke.

I couldn't believe how much interest our story was generating. And there was more to come.

A few months after my name went up in lights on the WPF website, I received a very interesting email. Scott Baskett is a documentary maker from Melbourne. He was amazed by the world-wide phenomenon that is sudoku and he was keen to do what he called a 'sudokumentary'. He wanted to know what I had to do as the Australian member, where I was holding the Australian Championship and when I'd be choosing the national team for the World Championship. He'd already been in contact with Hendrik.

When I explained to Scott why I had joined the WPF in the first place, he thought it was fantastic. One of the funniest things he'd ever heard. It was just the angle he was looking for. I kept in touch with Scott as things progressed and, before I knew it, Scott and his cameraman, Bayden Findlay, were flying to Perth to start shooting.

They filmed my interview at 6PR. They got comments from Steve Mills and interviewed Ryan. They spoke to Ted Sutherland about the thrill of being the first father since Mr Waugh to have two sons heading to India in the same Australian team.

Ryan was on fire. He lined up some great interviews for the sudokumentary, including one with the Lord Mayor of Perth. But the coup de grâce involved two of Australia's best known sportsmen.

Dean Cox is a ruckman with the West Coast Eagles. He spoke to Scott and Bayden and said that one of his biggest regrets was that AFL is not an international game. He wished he could play for Australia in his chosen sport, but knew he'd never get the chance.

The other key interview was with Nathan Sharpe, captain of the Emirates Western Force and a seventy-plus test veteran for the Wallabies. Unlike Dean, 'Sharpie' was able to speak at length about what it means to play for your country and about how proud he was to wear the green and gold.

The 'Members Equity Numbats' and the 'Wallabies', spoken in the same breath. It was fantastic.

I'd always planned on taking a camera with me to India. So when Scott asked if I could also take a mini DV, I didn't hesitate to say yes. They'd done a brilliant job getting background interviews in Perth and needed the footage I'd take in India to complete the project.

The proposal I put together for Paul and Members Equity must have been okay. He generously gave us a cash donation, as well as tickets to a number of events at Members Equity Stadium. If we sold them, we could keep the proceeds.

Sandy, Skiffo, Hamish and I were prepared to stump up the cash and pay for our trip to India, regardless of any financial support that might have come our way. Scott and Bayden had put their hands in their pockets to get to Perth. That was good enough for us.

We decided any money we received from Members Equity would go directly towards getting either Scott or Bayden to India so they could finish the sudokumentary. We were going anyway; having a professional cameraman come to document our adventure in perpetuity would be priceless.

We gave Scott the good news and the publicity machine rolled on. Interviews on 3AW, 4BC and 2UE followed, along with a story in *The Sunday Times* magazine and appearances on Channel Seven's *Today Tonight*, Channel Nine's *Today* show and the Channel Nine news.

My two boys were filmed as part of the *Today Tonight* segment and they made sure their classmates watched when it went to air. The next day, when I dropped them off at school, all the Year 2s were pointing and whispering, 'That's Matt's dad.'

I felt ten feet tall.

While the media frenzy continued, Sharan was training seven days a week and playing water polo for the Fremantle Marlins in the National League, a competition set up in a similar way to the AFL, minus the salaries and profile. There are two teams from Western Australia, five from New South Wales, two from Queensland, and one each from South Australia and Victoria.

The Marlins had won four of the past five national league titles. They were easily Western Australia's, if not Australia's, most successful provincial sports team. But the only TV or radio coverage Sharan received was when she was given a cameo role or a mention in the stories about the Australian Sudoku Team.

She didn't think it was fair that four bumbling fools were everywhere and that water polo was nowhere. I understood where she was coming from. But, as I explained, if she were playing a real game, like sudoku, her efforts might attract a bit more interest.

My bruises have nearly healed.

Chapter 15

Rocky Balboa

Despite all the noise we were making in the media, there was still disturbing silence in one area.

Hendrik.

I hadn't heard from him at all, which was completely out of character. I sent email after email, asking if he'd received the news about the Australian team. I sent emails asking if he'd received the emails asking if he'd received the news about the Australian team.

But I got nothing back.

I was beginning to worry. We'd all paid for our flights and our gear and told everyone we were going. I tried ringing Hendrik but couldn't get through. I rang the WPF headquarters in Germany, expressing my concern. I was getting desperate. Then, finally, some news.

Dear Member

As you may have noticed, for the past weeks communications with Hendrik Hardeman about the upcoming WSC in Goa have not been possible. I know he has been ill. So, in case you have been writing, please be patient a bit more. I am sure Hendrik will be in touch with you again shortly.

Nevertheless, just in case, you'd better wait with actually booking your flights for Goa until communications have been restored. This is surely just an over-reaction, but better safe than sorry.

You've got to be kidding me.

I emailed straight back and explained how we had already paid around $9000 in fares, all having taken cheap options that were non-refundable. While the powers that be were sympathetic, their response didn't exactly fill me with confidence:

Hi Mick,

The situation is like I described: we cannot come in contact with Hendrik, neither by phone nor by e-mail. Therefore the warning.

The qualifier for the Indian championship, organized by Hendrik as well is on soon and we are in contact with Indians who will participate there.

So on that day we will know for sure: if it is held, we will be able to communicate with Hendrik, and surely before that. If it is not held, we will probably need to decide to cancel the WSC in Goa.

Great. Just great.

I had no option but to tell the rest of the Australian team the news – the toughest email I'd ever sent. To say they were fuming is like saying Don Bradman could bat a bit. Sandy, in particular, was at a loss as to how an entire World Championship event could hinge on the health of one man.

We didn't know what to do. Did we cancel and consider the whole thing a good idea that went bad? Or did we go anyway and just have a holiday? Granted, it would be at a destination none of us wanted to go to, but with good company and cold beer, any destination can be a good one. So that's what we decided to do.

Then I had an idea.

Every situation you find yourself in is another opportunity. You can either make something of it or not. We decided to make something of it.

I sent an email to the WPF, informing the board that we were going, regardless of Hendrik's situation.

A few weeks after we'd announced the Australian team, Skiffo sat me down and said he needed to speak to me seriously about something.

'Mick,' he said. 'I know you blokes are treating this whole thing as a bit of a joke, and that's fair enough. But I *can* play. This is my one shot at a world title. I want to give it a real crack.'

He was right. How many people are actually given a shot at winning a world title? We had been. And Skiffo was going for it. He was Rocky Balboa up against Apollo Creed.

Just how much of an underdog he was came to light when he played a game of sudoku online, against Thomas Snyder, the defending world champion. Skiffo completed the game in twelve minutes twenty-seven seconds. He was ecstatic. He'd taken his A game into the arena and was riding high. This was exactly the form he wanted going into the World Championship.

Snyder did the same puzzle in one minute eighteen seconds.

So when it struck me that we might be the only team competing, I sent another email to the WPF. I put forward a proposition that, if accepted, would go down as one of the greatest come-from-behind victories in Australia's history.

This would be bigger than Kieren Perkins winning in Atlanta from lane eight. Bigger than *Australia II* coming from three–nil down to win the America's Cup.

I asked whether, if I ran a sudoku competition in Goa, the WPF would recognise it as an official World Sudoku Championship.

It was a fairly optimistic request, but we had nothing to lose. Neither did the WPF. Even though the competition would be on a very small scale, it would be better for them if the record books showed that a tournament took place. I felt it was a win-win proposition.

It seems they agreed.

Dear Mick

Good news you are going, and good idea to do something anyway. I am sure the WPF will have no problems to call it a WSC no matter what, which you can use for promotional things.

The positive response transformed our holiday in an instant. No longer were we just going to India for a few beers and some beach cricket. One of us would be coming home with the title of World Champion.

Skiffo's odds shortened from a 500/1 outsider to the 2/1-on short-priced favourite.

When the Wallabies won the 1991 Rugby World Cup against England, it took a while for their accomplishment to sink in. This was given a hurry-on when Sam Scott-Young stood up in the dressing room and shouted, 'Sam Scott-Young, World Champion!' One by one, the rest of his team mates followed, standing to make the same triumphant announcement about themselves.

That was going to be us. On form, Skiffo would win the individual world title and Australia was a shoo-in to win the team event, especially if we were the only participant. We were on the verge of glory; more than even we could possibly have imagined. We pictured double-page spreads in *New Idea*, invitations to celebrity golf days and autograph sessions at all the major shopping centres on our return.

Then we started thinking. Why settle for one of us winning a World title? If we're running the competition, we might as well split the World Sudoku Championship into different weight divisions. That way, we could all bring home a WPF world-title belt. Best of all, Skiffo could legitimately call himself the undisputed Heavy Weight Champion of the World.

Every cloud has a silver lining. This one was made of gold.

I was almost disappointed when Hendrik made contact again. He was back, the tournament was back and we were back to 500/1 long shots.

When the long-awaited tournament schedule was released, the seriousness of what we were getting ourselves into became apparent.

> *MONDAY 14 April: Arrival all day, optional excursion, welcome dinner + Q&A.*
> *TUESDAY 15 April: Competition all day.*
> *WEDNESDAY 16 April: Competition, play-offs, press conference, farewell party.*
> *THURSDAY 17 April: Departure all day, optional excursion.*

We immediately began our taper.

The list of competing nations was also finalised, the scale of the event and the popularity of the game becoming crystal clear:

Australia	Italy
Bangladesh	Japan
Belarus	Korea
Belgium	Luxembourg
Bulgaria	Netherlands
Canada	Philippines
China	Poland
Chinese Taipei	Portugal
Czech Republic	Serbia
Denmark	Slovakia
Estonia	Spain
France	Switzerland
Germany	Turkey
Hungary	United Kingdom
India	United States

Which basically meant Australia's world ranking looked like dropping out of the top twenty-nine for the first time.

I told my sons how many teams were playing. They responded by saying my World Championship was better than the ones their mum played in because hers only had twelve nations taking part.

I always knew they were bright.

After looking at our list of opponents, we decided to also take across a cricket bat and ball, to take on the Indians and the poms at the end of each day's play. We would do our bit for international relations and, hopefully, restore a bit of Australian pride. Although, whether elite sudoku players were into cricket remained to be seen.

It was an exciting time and I actually started feeling nervous. I would be carrying the hopes of our nation at an official World Championship. What if I embarrassed Australia? What if I was completely humiliated? What if I became the laughing stock of the sudoku world?

Theodore Roosevelt was the twenty-sixth President of the United States of America. I'm not sure if he used a speech writer but he's credited with one of my favourite quotes:

> *It is not the critic who counts; not the man who points out how the strong man stumbles, or where the doer of deeds could have done them better. The credit belongs to the man who is actually in the arena, whose face is marred by dust and sweat and blood, who strives valiantly; who errs and comes short again and again; because there is not effort without error and shortcomings; but who does actually strive to do the deed; who knows the great enthusiasm, the great devotion, who spends himself in a worthy cause, who at the best knows in the end the triumph of high achievement and who at the worst, if he fails, at least he fails while daring greatly. So that his place shall never be with those cold and timid souls who know neither victory nor defeat.*

Reading those words again cheered me up immensely. I knew that I might fail, but I would fail while daring greatly. And, regardless of how I went, I would return home as the most capped Australian sudoku player in history.

I couldn't wait.

CHAPTER 16

Damn you, Andrew Symonds

The subcontinent can be a daunting place at the best of times. Now, we were about to head there on the back of one of the greatest controversies in Australian sport. A controversy that strained relations between the two countries like never before.

Andrew Symonds is a champion cricketer for Queensland and Australia. A more than useful bowler and powerful batsman, he's dynamic and aggressive, with the ability to win a game on his own with either bat or ball.

A few months before we were due to depart, the dark-skinned, dreadlock-wearing Symonds was the target of racist abuse during the fifth one-day international against India in Vadodara: the crowd made monkey chants while he was fielding on the boundary. While it made the news, it was denied by the Indian authorities and largely ignored in the hope that it would just go away.

It didn't.

The tension kept building and it all came to a head in January 2008, when the Indians toured Australia in what was touted as one of the most anticipated test series in years.

Sydney's famous SCG was the venue for the second test. Indian bowler Harbhajan Singh was batting with the great Sachin Tendulkar. There'd been quite a bit of sledging throughout the match and tensions were starting to rise. At the completion of the 116th over, a verbal altercation took place between Harbhajan and Symonds. This in itself wasn't unusual. But what happened next was. Instead of play continuing, it came to a grinding halt. Ricky Ponting approached umpires Steve Bucknor and Mark Benson and made an official complaint, alleging that Harbhajan Singh called Andrew Symonds a 'big monkey'.

A four-hour hearing was held at the SCG the following evening, with ICC match referee Mike Procter finding Harbhajan guilty under rule 3.3 of the ICC Code of Conduct, which refers to players or team officials 'using language or gestures that offends, insults, humiliates, intimidates, threatens, disparages or vilifies another person on the basis of that person's race, religion, gender, colour, descent, or national or ethic origin'.

He suspended Harbhajan for three matches.

The Indians were furious.

In Kolkata and Kanpur, effigies of the two umpires were set alight in protest. The Australian team also came under attack, with the Press Trust of India reporting one fan as saying, 'The Aussies don't play the game in the right spirit. They claim catches when they know the ball has bounced.' The attack continued, with *The Indian Express* posting a photo on its website of a fan in Kolkata holding a sign that read, 'Ponting is the most coward and cheater captain of Australia.'

It was getting ugly. What started out as an international incident looked like escalating into an international crisis.

The Indians lodged an appeal. They were so angry with the decision handed down by the match referee that they held world cricket to ransom and threatened to abandon their multi-million dollar tour of Australia unless the suspension was overturned.

Over the next few days, it became increasingly clear that the Indian cricket board was the sport's most powerful national governing body. The Indians held their ground and were quite prepared to, literally, pick up their bat and ball and go home. While the ICC could have stuck to its guns and showed that it was the one in charge, it eventually bowed to the pressure and made a number of significant concessions, which satisfied the Indians and allowed the tour to continue.

Harbhajan's charge was downgraded from racial abuse to using offensive language. He was fined fifty per cent of his match fee. In addition, Steve Bucknor, who had incurred the wrath of the Indians for making a number of errors in the Australians' favour, was stood down from officiating at the third and fourth tests in Perth and Adelaide respectively.

Relations between the two countries remained frosty at best and the last place any Australian team wanted to tour was India. We wondered how we would be received when we arrived in Mumbai, decked out in our national blazers. For a brief moment we actually considered not travelling in our Number 1s, but knowing it would be our one and only time, we decided to risk it. We were proud to be heading off to play for Australia and wanted the world to know it.

Standing at Perth airport, fully kitted out, was a good feeling. It was hard not to smile as we watched other passengers staring at the national crest and embroidery on our blazers, trying to figure out who we were. When they realised they were looking at the Australian Sudoku Team en route to the World Sudoku Championship in India, they walked off with a 'wow, they must be clever' kind of expression. I savoured that while I could.

Sandy and Hamish were heading to India from Switzerland and Bali respectively, so it was just Skiffo and me leaving from Perth. We were joined by Bayden from the 'sudokumentary' crew, who captured our every move on camera and made us look very important indeed.

Our bags were checked in by a lady of Indian descent – I wasn't sure if this was an omen. We puffed out our chests and pushed our left breasts towards the operator, making sure she could see the crest and that we were part of an Australian team. She wasn't impressed at all, and just went about her business.

'Excuse me, ma'am,' Skiffo began. 'Our travel agent said to see whether there was any chance we might be able to get an upgrade because we're part of an Australian team.'

She slowly raised her eyes to us before returning her attention to the screen. She tapped a few keys and replied, 'There's nothing on the system.'

'No, we were just told to ask if it was possible to get an upgrade. We're in the Australian team, heading to the World Championship.' We were sounding desperate but we didn't care. Neither did she. She pushed our boarding passes towards us.

Row 51.

It was obviously because of the Andrew Symonds incident. We decided she must have been a cricket fan and hadn't forgiven the Australians for their treatment of Harbhajan. Seating us way up the back of the plane, just next to the toilets, was her idea of revenge.

There was no point in complaining, so we made our way upstairs, filled in our departure cards and went through customs. The customs officer was the guy we wanted to have allocating the seats:

'G'day, fellas!' he said. 'I saw you blokes on TV. Great stuff. Congratulations. Good luck over there. Hope you do really well.'

Then, when he saw our boarding passes, the comment that would have broken weaker men:

'Thought they might have given you an upgrade.'

At least we had membership to the lounge, so we waltzed in and headed straight for the complimentary food and beverages. The place was packed with surfers who'd just competed at the Margaret River Masters. They looked a real rabble. A handsome rabble. We were pristine in comparison.

I don't know if it's due to my upbringing, but I can't help taking free stuff. Growing up, I always had a roof over my head and food on my plate, but I certainly wasn't brought up in a home flooded with wealth. There was a lot of love, just not a lot of money. So the Qantas lounge, with its complimentary drinks and self-serve snack bar, was my kind of place.

Being in the lounge reminded me of my involvement with a big international golf tournament held in Perth at the Vines Resort. It's been known by a few names over the years, but when I was involved it was known as the Heineken Classic. One year I had the pleasure of caddying for a journeyman Victorian golfer by the name of Steve Porch, Marty Roebuck's brother-in-law. I'm a terrible golfer but, like most people, I can appreciate any sport when it's played well. Caddying for Steve was a real eye-opener. And it was the perfect gig for someone like me who has a penchant for taking things they don't have to pay for.

When it comes to glamorous professions, being a professional golfer is just short of being a rock star. They tour the world and make obscene amounts of money. Apparently. Steve, though, was in the other ninety-nine per cent of professional golfers. The ones who struggle through various tours, where every putt they make means another meal they can afford.

Steve would come across each year from his home state with two other professionals and play the four-week West Australian circuit. Unlike the top-tier professionals who can afford to pay for their own flights and accommodation but never have to, Steve and his mates had to cover all their own expenses. So the three of them would sleep on the floor at our place in Claremont, which meant that for one month every year, we'd have eight guys living together. It was always very cool, though, being able to say we had professional golfers staying with us. They were great blokes and adapted very quickly to our little world.

Every year he tried to, Steve qualified for the Heineken Classic. Golfers who play in it are supposed to pay a wage to their caddies, but because his tour generally operated at a loss, I always offered my services for free. I was no use whatsoever when it came to club selection or reading greens. I had no idea what I was doing but I could carry his clubs and that's all he needed. I guess you get what you pay for.

As a sports fan who always enjoys being on the inside, it was an absolute thrill being a caddy. I was given a uniform, which included two collared shirts, two pairs of shorts, two pairs of socks and a cap. I'd sit in the change room before we'd tee off and get kitted up. It was exciting, rubbing shoulders with professionals who did this for a living. There was food and drink for the caddies, so I used to stuff my face before we went out. I wasn't necessarily hungry, but it was there and it was free.

The Heineken Classic was always held in February. If you've ever been to Perth in February, you'll know it's generally the hottest time of the year there. The Vines course is a fair way east of Perth, so you normally feel the cooling effects of the sea breeze about three days after it's come in.

On the first tee, the announcer would welcome the playing pair and the crowd in the stand would sit in silence, then applaud when the ball was sent flying down the fairway. You can't appreciate how far these guys hit the ball until you actually watch it fly off the club head and then have to walk to where it lands. Carrying a heavy bag with more clubs than I knew what to do with made the distance seem even further.

If there's one thing I learnt about pro golfers, it's that they walk fast. They tee off, hand the club to their caddy, then go. I'd be left back at the tee, wiping the head down. Then I'd have to put the club back in the bag, lift it up and run the thirty metres or so to catch up to Steve.

At every tee, there were bottles of Gatorade in big Eskies of ice. I wasn't necessarily thirsty but they were there and they were free. So I took one. At every hole.

By about the seventh, I couldn't possibly drink any more. At the eighth, ninth and tenth, I had to duck behind trees to relieve myself. I swear my urine was orange.

Back on the course, I was constantly in awe of Steve. He'd use the sprinkler heads as markers and, with his score card, work out exactly how far it was to the pin. A metre either way would determine which club he chose. That's how precise these golfers are. Being around him gave me a far greater appreciation of the skills required and the technical aspects of a very difficult game.

As the day wore on, the temperature rose steadily. I think of all the times I caddied there, the coolest day was about forty-two degrees. I would dip the towel I was wiping the clubs with into the Esky and put it over my head. I'd psych myself up while Steve addressed the ball, then switch into game mode. Grab the club, wipe it, put it in the bag, pick up the bag and start walking. I was counting down the holes, praying that I would be able to hang on. My feet were killing me and I was exhausted. And it was only the first day.

For one of the rounds, Steve was partnered with Rodger Davis, a well-known Australian golfer who spent twenty-nine weeks between 1987 and 1992 ranked in the world top ten. We had a sizeable gallery follow us around and I was soaking up the atmosphere. The eighteenth was surrounded on three sides by grandstands and corporate tents, which were full of people. Some of them were golf fans, others were more like me – people who had just come for the free stuff. Regardless, it was a fairly impressive sight.

Steve was about to putt to finish off his round. I was holding the pin, looking around at the sea of faces.

'Mick.'

I was thinking what a beautiful day it was. Thinking there must be three or four hundred people there, all watching me.

'Mick.'

Wow. How cool is this?

'MICK!'

Steve had been calling out to me to remove the pin. I was so caught up in the moment I didn't hear him until he had to shout. He missed the putt.

At the end of the day's play, we went to hand in his card. By this stage, the bag I was carrying felt like it weighed about 200 kilos. I didn't want to embarrass myself, so I had to grit my teeth and hold my form until I reached the sanctuary of the dressing rooms. It was a bit like how you suck your gut in coming out of the surf when you see a group of girls heading towards you. When I made it inside, I dropped the bag to the floor and slumped against the wall. I was spent. I had just enough energy to reach across and grab a chocolate bar, a sandwich and another Gatorade. Only because they were free.

Back in the Qantas lounge I helped myself to another piece of chocolate cake as our flight was finally called, and swallowed the last bit just before boarding. We made a casual comment to the stewardess about the possibility of being upgraded, but, again, it fell on deaf ears. We had hoped we could get on and turn left. Instead, we were ushered right to make the long trek towards the rear. A few passengers who'd been following our story wished us all the best. We thanked them, then kept on walking.

And walking.

CHAPTER 17
The breakthrough

Inflight entertainment systems have come a long way in the past few years. Especially on international flights. We all had our own TV screens, which were located in the backs of the seats in front of us. We had a choice of films and the ability to control when each one started.

I decided to go for what I thought would be one of those motivational sports films, as a way of pumping myself up for the World Championship, which was less than forty-eight hours away. I chose *Mr Woodcock*, a film starring Billy Bob Thornton, who plays the role of a high school basketball coach.

I was wrong. Very wrong.

I probably should have gone to sleep but had a huge choice of complimentary movies to watch. And I didn't want to miss out on the free meal either.

About an hour out of Singapore, Skiffo pulled out his trusty book of sudoku puzzles to get in some practice. That's why he was the captain. Then it hit me. Here I was, on my way to India to represent Australia at the World Sudoku Championship, and I still hadn't completed a sudoku puzzle. I figured if I was ever going to start, now was as good a time as any. I grabbed the inflight magazine from the seat pocket in front of me, turned to the page with the sudoku puzzles and announced my intention to the skipper.

He was proud of me. He also said it was important I start getting used to the pressure of competition. So he reached into his seat pocket and grabbed *his* inflight magazine. It was on. Me versus the skipper. Australian captain versus Australian vice-captain. Two of the greatest sudoku minds in history going head to head. If there had been tickets available, it would have been a sellout.

My first attempt was a disaster but I consoled myself with the fact that it was my first-ever go. We moved to the second puzzle. I started off strongly and began feeling confident. 'This isn't too bad,' I thought. 'I might actually be okay at this.'

I got to within about six numbers when it all fell in a heap. You think you're flying, then you discover that the next number you write has already been written in the same column. It's too hard to find where your mistake is, so you concede. It wasn't looking good. I was on the wrong side of two from two.

The skipper sensed I was struggling and that he needed to give me a lift. So he returned to his book of puzzles and we went to the chapter containing the easy ones.

'Here, try one of these,' he said in a calm, comforting voice.

So I did. And I stuffed up again. I didn't start crying but I wasn't far off. My confidence was at an all-time low. How could I expect to do world-standard puzzles when I couldn't even do an easy one?

The skipper pulled me aside and gave me some pointers. He told me not to try to get rows or columns out straightaway. He told me to look for the number that appears the most often, then try to work out where that same number goes in the other blocks of nine. He said to work the blocks first. The rows and columns would look after themselves.

I learned more about sudoku in that one-minute pep talk than I had in an entire lifetime. I turned to another easy puzzle and began. I looked for the most common number. Worked out where else it had to go. Worked the blocks first. Then worried about the rows and columns. It was all coming together. I was in the zone. I couldn't believe it. Only three numbers left. Two numbers. One number. I'd done it. I'd finished my first-ever sudoku puzzle. I was elated. The skipper was elated. He shook my hand. It was the breakthrough we needed.

I was on a roll. I'd completed a puzzle. There was no stopping me.

CHAPTER 18

Damn you, Andrew Symonds (Part II)

I would have no problem holidaying in Singapore airport. It's like a massive department store, only cleaner. And it has those long travelators that make you feel like you're the Six Million Dollar Man. You take long strides and speed past the mere mortals who've decided that a walk on solid ground will do them good after being seated in the air for so long.

As we stepped onto the moving footpath, a voice behind us asked the question we'd been longing for:

'Are you the Australian Sudoku Team?'

We tried to act all cool but were visibly excited by being recognised in a foreign country. We spun around.

'Yes, we are!'

It was the principal of a primary school in Perth. He'd seen us on TV and wished us all the best on behalf of the kids. It wasn't a buxom groupie, but it was a start.

We had to change planes and get new boarding passes for the flight from Singapore to Mumbai. While we were still ticketed with Qantas, the carrier was Jet Airways. We caught the skytrain to the next terminal and found the check-in desk.

Once again, we puffed out our chests and turned our left breasts towards the attendant, who also happened to be of Indian descent.

'Excuse me, ma'am,' Skiffo began, almost by rote. 'Our travel agent said to see whether there was any chance we might be able to get an upgrade because we're part of an Australian team.'

She looked at a couple of screens, then shook her head. 'There's nothing on the system.'

'No, we were just told to ask if it was possible to get an upgrade. We're in the Australian team, heading to the World Championship.'

'I'm sorry. I can't help you.'

This whole Andrew Symonds thing was getting out of control. I felt like telling her to just let it go, but figured the best way to improve relations was to take our boarding passes, smile and thank her for trying.

So that's what we did.

We had some time to kill, so Skiffo decided to get himself a massage. Not a happy-ending massage, a foot massage. As we approached one of the many establishments offering the service, we saw the manager sitting down outside the entrance. He was on his break and it looked like he was reading. As we got closer, we realised he was playing sudoku. It really is the world game.

That lady at the check-in counter obviously hated Andrew Symonds even more than we thought. She had told us we had a couple of hours before our flight to Mumbai but it turned out there was only about forty minutes. By chance, there was a departure screen outside the massage parlour and our flight was already flashing Final Call. Bayden and I raced inside and grabbed Skiffo, who was forced to end his massage unsatisfied. It wasn't the first time.

You hear some scary stories about overseas airlines but Jet Airways couldn't have been better. Either the plane was brand-new or they had the world's best cleaning and maintenance staff in aviation history. It was spotless. And, more importantly, spacious. The TV screens on the seat backs were enormous and the inflight entertainment included sudoku and an Indian version of 'Who Wants to Be a Millionaire?'. As a couple of easily amused Australians, we were pretty content.

I expected the worst when we landed in Mumbai but I was pleasantly surprised. It was quite cold initially but the further we moved inside the terminal, the hotter it became. That was mainly because the big stand-up air-conditioners lining the walkways became fewer and fewer before disappearing altogether.

I thought going through customs would be mayhem but it all moved very smoothly. There were lots of people arriving but there also must have been about thirty booths open where officers were checking passports. A man sat on an old bar stool at the front of the line and when a booth was free, he'd call its number out and point you in the right direction. 17…29…4…18…2…11. It was like a big game of bingo.

The mayhem started the moment we stepped outside.

India is one big culture shock. It was oppressively hot and there were people everywhere. We had to step around beggars and over homeless people who were sound asleep on the footpath, oblivious to the noise. When we exited the terminal, we were met by a wall of people holding cards with passenger names written on them. We tried to find one with 'Australian Sudoku Team' but had no luck.

The moment you pass the pack of waiting drivers, you're fair game. Scouts approach you on behalf of other drivers, who race towards you when they get the nod. Before you have a chance to say no, they've taken your bags and are heading towards a vehicle that would be deemed unroadworthy in any other country.

The Andrew Symonds effect continued when a man asked us where we were from. So much for worrying about whether we should wear our blazers. We told him we were from Australia. He then proceeded to charge us the equivalent of what was probably his whole day's pay to lift one of our bags into the back of a beat-up van. The driver refused to depart until we paid the handler.

We left the airport and immediately felt as though we'd been transported into the chase scene of a Bollywood-style James Bond film. There was traffic everywhere but the driver was speeding like he was on an open road. He zig-zagged and weaved his way through the seething mass of humanity, past logs, dogs, potholes, buses, tuk-tuks, pedestrians, and cabs that looked like they had rolled off the showroom floor back in the 1930s. Then, when he got within an inch of the car in front, he would slam on the brakes. It was a pattern that continued for the next twenty minutes until we were delivered, pale and frightened, to our hotel.

We handed over what we later discovered was close to his week's wage for the privilege. Then paid the best part of an average Indian monthly wage for one night's accommodation.

Andrew Symonds owes me.

Our connecting flight to Goa left at 6am so we were on the road early. The traffic was nowhere near as hectic as it had been the night before, but it was still far busier than anything I'd ever experienced at that time of day. The domestic airport was packed. India's population is more than a billion. We didn't doubt it.

There were people everywhere, workers and passengers. 'Organised chaos' is putting a positive spin on it. All the bags are placed on one conveyor belt, so as you watch yours disappear, it's a matter of crossing your fingers and hoping they get to where they're supposed to go.

We passed our hand luggage through the X-ray machine, then stood on what looked like a milk crate while a security guard squeezed our buttocks and rubbed his hand up and down our legs. Then it was just a matter of finding a seat and a TV monitor that would indicate which gate we'd depart from.

The first bit was easy. The second, impossible. Mumbai domestic airport is more like a train station. There are ten departure gates and workers manually slide the flight information sign in and out of the gate. At one stage there were ten different flights scheduled to depart in the space of fifteen minutes.

We saw the board for departures to Goa inserted and made our way through. It was a journey of about ten metres and led us outside. There were planes everywhere, with no pattern to where they were. It was like each pilot had said to the air traffic controller, 'Where do you want me to put it?' and the response had been 'It doesn't matter. Anywhere you can find a spot.'

Our bus arrived to take us to our plane. We boarded, sat down, stood up and disembarked. People have been on angry bulls longer than we were on that bus. The trip lasted no more than eight seconds and covered less than twenty metres. There was no need whatsoever for us to catch a bus to the plane. But who were we to argue?

The conditions on the internal flight from Mumbai to Goa were primitive to say the least. The boarding pass had a flight number but no seat allocation. You sat anywhere you wanted. The centre aisle was so narrow that the flight attendants bumped you every time they passed. There was no meal, just a hot towel and a thick, sickly sweet lemon drink.

I took one sip but that was all I could handle. It was free, but even I have my limits.

CHAPTER 19

Dog's balls

I've only ever felt like a rock star once. That was in Pattaya, Thailand. I walked past a bar and about a dozen attractive young girls started yelling and waving. I looked around to make sure they weren't trying to get the attention of someone behind me – I'd embarrassed myself in similar circumstances before. When I realised I was the only one there, I walked over to them and was swamped. They told me I was handsome, wanted me to sit with them and have a drink. I couldn't believe it. I'd finally found a place where people who look like me were considered hot.

I was brought back to reality about ten seconds later when I saw them do exactly the same thing to the next bloke who walked past. And the next. Sadly, I realised it wasn't my good looks and personality they were after.

The reaction we received when we landed in Goa wasn't quite as enthusiastic, but we still felt special. We were kitted up in our casual Australian team uniform – polo shirts and walk shorts – and met by a stranger holding up a sign that read: 'WELCOME DELEGATES WOLRD SODOKU CHAMPIONSHIP'. We weren't dodging paparazzi or fighting our way through hordes of autograph hunters and well-wishers, but I couldn't help feeling that we were slightly important, that at least a few people were looking at us. I'm sure they weren't, but it was all part of the fantasy.

Our hotel, the Holiday Inn at Mobor Beach, was doubling as the venue for the tournament. The WPF had arranged transfers from Goa airport, so we gave our bags to the porter and followed him to an old bus. It was a beauty, with a purple interior and dark blue curtains, all pulled closed.

Bayden, who was sweating profusely and had predicted that he wouldn't stop until we were back in Australia, was busy filming.

Arriving anywhere when you're on tour is good fun, mainly because you're in unfamiliar territory and you never know what's going to happen next. Those same levels of uncertainty apply to your knowledge of the opposition. At my level, I never knew whether we were going to win by fifty or get belted by the same margin.

In 1978, Manly and Wests – rugby league teams from opposite sides of Sydney – travelled to Melbourne to play in an exhibition game at the start of the season. Manly, based on the northern beaches, was known as the Silvertails. Wests, from the working-class western suburbs, was known as the Fibros, after the material many of the houses in that area were made from. They were the fiercest of rivals and their legendary on-field battles featured some of the most blatant violence ever witnessed on the field of play.

Put simply, the two teams hated each other.

Although aware of the animosity, the NSW Rugby League booked the teams on the same plane for the flight to Victoria. Wests players were under instructions not to talk to the opposition, which fuelled the tension that already existed. The teams were also booked into the same hotel, but Manly decided to move. Wests then felt that the Silvertails thought they were too good to associate with the Fibros, so by game time, all hell was set to break loose.

And it did.

Off-the-ball acts of thuggery were commonplace and a number of Manly players needed hospital treatment.

The rivalry between the Silvertails and the Fibros continued during the 1980s but it wasn't restricted to senior-level rugby league.

I was a member of the South West Zone representative side at that time, and we were set to play a game against the Northern Zone. Our team was made up of players from the southern and western districts of Sydney, places such as Parramatta, St George and Eastwood. The opposition contained players from teams such as Manly, Warringah and other north-of-the-harbour areas.

Our coach was looking for a way to motivate us before we ran out, and decided that if the rich versus poor was good enough for Manly and Wests, it was good enough for us.

Spots in the Sydney Under 18 team were up for grabs, so most of the guys were pretty fired up anyway. But that didn't stop the coach. He started off telling us how the guys from Manly all drove nice cars, had good-looking girlfriends and lived in nice houses. How they thought we lived in fibro houses. How they all thought they were better than us.

Just as the coach's speech was building to a crescendo, one of our players shot up his hand.

'Excuse me, coach,' he said.

The coach stopped. 'Yes,' he replied, somewhat miffed that his Churchillian address had been interrupted.

'You *do* live in a fibro house.'

We all burst out laughing. The coach didn't know what to say. The match official knocked on the dressing-room door and told us it was time to take the field, and we were all still giggling as we ran out.

We lost the game but it remains one of my career highlights.

We didn't exactly have the same history together as Manly and Wests, but I still felt a bit uneasy when I discovered the Australians would be sharing the bus with the Dutch and Belgian Sudoku Teams. While I tried to stare them down and gain that mental edge, they just looked bewildered by an Australian team dressed in matching uniforms and accompanied by a cameraman.

Bayden used the opportunity to interview some of our opponents and he was quick to report back when one of the Dutch players said that we didn't 'look like puzzlers'. It was like Bayden had decided to become our team psychologist and was already starting to get us fired up. I pictured him pasting up motivational messages on our bedroom walls before each day's play.

We pondered the Dutch player's observation and didn't know how to take it – whether as an insult or a compliment. I went on the offensive and took it as an insult. I was angry. Fired up. How dare they say that. Skiffo asked why I was never in that frame of mind when I was playing rugby. He was right. I pulled my head in.

The bus trip was an experience in itself. I'd never met legitimate international sudoku players before and there I was, somewhere in India, sitting alongside them on a bus straight out of the Partridge Family, on my way to the World Championship.

Not only was that my first glimpse of an international-standard puzzler, it was my first glimpse into the life of an international-standard puzzler. While Skiffo and I pulled back the curtains so we could take in the scenery of a place we'd never been before, the Dutch and the Belgian competitors kept their curtains closed and did sudoku puzzles for the entire trip.

I had been under the impression that Goa was a resort town, like Terrigal in New South Wales or Broome in Western Australia. I had thought it would be a short ten-minute journey there. As I soon discovered, Goa is actually a small state, about one and a half times bigger than the Australian Capital Territory, covering almost 4000 square kilometres.

It has an interesting history, having been ruled by the colonial Portuguese for more than 450 years, and it presents a real mix of cultures. It has European-style central squares and Indian bazaars, while Portuguese churches share their walls with those of Hindu temples.

We passed a number of small villages as we made our way towards Mobor Beach. The road was only one lane wide and full of pot-holes, but somehow our bus found room to overtake a tractor while another bus of similar size approached from the other direction. We shut our eyes and hoped for the best.

Life in this part of the world seemed very simple and made our life in Australia appear opulent in comparison. We passed a tarpaulin tied to a tree by the side of the road, which had a family of five sitting beneath it. The tarpaulin was their home. They smiled and waved as we drove by. I imagined what it must be like to live there. There I was, wanting a better home, a bigger yard, a swimming pool and a new car. I wanted everything and was miserable because I didn't have it. They had nothing but seemed happy. I wondered who was better off.

Further down the road, an old man stood behind a bench with a cage full of chickens on it. He reached in, grabbed a bird, held it on the table and, with one swift strike of a machete, cut its head off. He put the bird to the side and grabbed another. It was just a part of everyday life in downtown Goa.

I didn't know whether to be excited or nervous at the prospect of meeting Hendrik for the first time. I felt like I knew him already because of all our email correspondence, but a part of me was a bit worried as to his reaction if he discovered the truth behind our selection process. He'd put a heap of work into organising the tournament and the last thing I wanted was for Hendrik to think that I thought the whole thing was a big joke. I certainly didn't feel that way. I had a lot of respect for him and for the competition and I was here to do the best I could for my country.

I'm not real good with conflict so I figured the best way to deal with the situation was to avoid him altogether for as long as I could. But that plan came undone the moment Skiffo and I walked up the stairs and into the Holiday Inn.

A tall, wiry man dressed in black and sporting a smooth, shaved head approached us and held out his hand. 'I'm Hendrik,' he said.

The moment caught me by surprise and I felt genuinely excited to see him. 'Hendrik!' I replied, like I'd been re-united with a long-lost friend.

We introduced ourselves but instead of hugs and warm embraces, he proffered a polite hello then excused himself. He was gone before I had a chance to put down my bag. I guess he had more important things to worry about than exposing my charade.

It was already stinking hot when we arrived at the Holiday Inn, just after 9am. It was listed as a five-star hotel. It probably was twenty years ago. We couldn't check in until later that afternoon, so we left our bags at reception, then headed down for some breakfast. There was a decent spread laid on but I stuck with the Indian cuisine I was familiar with – Corn Flakes, orange juice and toast. Absolutely everything was labelled either vegetarian or non-vegetarian, from the bread to the eggs to the fruit. It must have been someone's job to do this, and they had done it extremely well.

Hamish and Sandy had arrived the day before and, while they had promised they'd do their very best not to have a big night, Skiffo had to find their room number, then go and knock on their door to get them up. They looked dusty but it was fantastic to see them. For the first time since those historic national titles, the Australian Sudoku Team was finally together. We were no longer four individuals. We were a cohesive unit, ready to take on the world.

The Dutch guy had been right, though. We stood out like dog's balls. Apart from a couple of specimens who looked like small bears, only more hairy, the majority of puzzlers we saw were slightly built with pale complexions. A high proportion of them wore socks with sandals and had their pants up well above their navels.

But I soon discovered they were not that different from me.

I've always liked wearing event T-shirts, whether they're from the Australian Surf Lifesaving Championships, the Dubai 7s or anything in between. The puzzle community seemed to be the same. As I sat in the foyer of the Holiday Inn, I saw puzzlers wearing T-shirts from a range of different national and international sudoku championships. The most impressive was the one that read: '24 Hour Puzzle Tournament. Competitor'. That's hard core. I figured those guys must have been puzzling's equivalent of someone who'd finished the Hawaiian Iron Man and had the shirt to prove it.

The hotel was booked out and, despite the large number of guests, it was quite easy to see who was there for the tournament. They were the ones doing puzzles. By the pool, on the lounges, in the lobby. It's like an addiction. We talk of 'pack-a-day' smokers. These were 'book-a-day' puzzlers. At no stage were they without one in their hands. Even at the breakfast table, they did puzzles in between bites. We couldn't help but overhear some of their conversations. There was nothing about the English Premier League, the NBA, the NFL or whether New Zealand will ever win another rugby world cup. It was all about puzzles, which ones they preferred, and updates on the new variations they were inventing.

No amount of practice was going to help us, so we decided to grab a couple of taxis and head into town for some lunch. We asked the concierge if there were any decent Indian restaurants around and he told us there was a terrific one in Panaji. That sounded good to us. The cabbie was pretty happy too, because Panaji was about an hour away.

You never really get used to overtaking on a single-lane road in the path of an oncoming truck. Maybe that's why there were so many shrines on the side of the road. Our driver blessed himself as we passed each one. It was a nice gesture but it didn't exactly fill me with confidence.

We arrived at the Delhi Darbar Restaurant and Bar and were pleasantly surprised to discover there was a special on – buy three pints of Kingfisher beer, get one free. It was a good start. Hamish and I have what we like to call 'sensitive palates', so we ordered chicken and cashews with steamed rice. Skiffo, Sandy and Bayden were a little more adventurous and ended up with something that was hot going in and would be the same going out. The food was delicious and, for some reason, we all found it highly amusing to be in India eating in an Indian restaurant.

Skiffo was the first to break the seal and when he returned he was positively ashen. I decided to investigate the reason for his distressed state and was equally shocked when I saw a man hanging around the toilets. He greeted you when you walked in, pointed you towards the trough, turned the tap on when you were done and pulled the paper out of the towel dispenser. He basically did everything except hold your johnson. It was one of those cultural differences I could do without.

Our drivers waited for us while we ate, then dropped us back to the Holiday Inn, so we could finally check in. Unpacking all our gear felt great, just like any other tour I'd been on. Only this time, all my gear had Australia written on it. I put a few things in my drawers but left the rest in my bag. I carefully unpacked my blazer and hung it alongside Skiffo's in the cupboard.

I found myself standing there, staring at it. I looked at the crest. That was *my* Australian blazer. It was hard to believe. I'd waited all my life to represent my country. And there I was, only one day away from actually doing it. Tomorrow couldn't come quickly enough.

CHAPTER 20

Mark Skiffington, Captain of Australia

The Olympic Games have re-defined the meaning of 'Opening Ceremony'. So when we heard there would be one for the World Sudoku Championship, we were pretty excited. It would be our chance to announce our arrival on sudoku's world stage and our first appearance as an Australian team at an official function.

We returned from lunch and had a couple of cool beers at Sam's Beach Shack, a friendly little establishment located in front of our hotel. We would have preferred cold beers but, for some reason, the concept of beer below room temperature hasn't caught on in Mobor. We did our best to help educate the staff and, in the nicest possible way, sent several rounds back to the fridge. We'd come a long way to represent our country and didn't want a little thing like warm beer to upset our preparation.

When the time came for us to get showered and changed, the temperature had dropped to thirty-nine degrees with a humidity level of just over ninety per cent. Not exactly the weather you want when you're stepping out in a blazer, long pants and a tie, but we didn't care. It could have been forty-nine degrees and we still would have worn it all exactly the same way – top button done up on the shirt and both buttons done up on the blazer.

It was something very special to see each other dressed in our Number 1s for the first time. Our warm handshakes communicated exactly how we all felt.

We took representing our country extremely seriously. Sweat was pouring down our backs but there was no way we would loosen our ties or take off our blazers. Which is why we found it surprising to see a rather large individual of Asian descent, devoid of muscle tone, sitting at the American team table with his shirt off. This was a significant moment – our first glimpse of a physique we now refer to as 'puzzler's body'.

We found out later that the shirtless one was Wei-Hwa Huang, one of America's best puzzlers. We also found out that he thought we looked liked 'saps' when we first walked in. That was about as big an insult as he could possibly have given, and when we heard what he'd said, we all considered making this World Sudoku Championship the first full-contact event in the game's history.

Seating at the dinner was arranged according to country. When we saw a table with AUSTRALIA written on the placard, our chests puffed out even further. We couldn't wipe the smiles off our faces. Some things just feel right and this was one of them. We ordered a round of Kingfishers, then made our way to the buffet to carbo-load for the following day's competition.

The ceremony was scheduled to finish at 9pm. By 8.50pm nothing had happened. A couple of guys – one who looked suspiciously like Ishant Sharma, the young Indian right-arm quick – had been playing guitars, backed by an electronic drum machine. So much for the fireworks and dancing girls. Finally, Hendrik appeared and took the microphone. He was not what you'd call a lengthy talker. He welcomed everyone along, then asked for a representative from each team to come up and say a few words.

We didn't realise it, but in the world of international sudoku, the captain is more like a non-playing manager. In Australian sport, the captain is revered, and that's how it was with our team. Hendrik invited the speakers to go up in alphabetical order, which meant Australia was first. None of us knew what to do and no one was particularly keen to do it. So we had a vote and it was unanimous. Skiffo was to be the one to do the speaking. We pumped him up and told him it was a responsibility that came with the title, so up he went.

'Good evening, ladies and gentleman. My name is Mark Skiffington and I'm the captain of Australia.'

Even if he hadn't said another word, this would still have been the greatest thing I had ever heard.

Responding to our cheers, he continued with all the polish of a seasoned professional. In his own inimitable style, he waxed lyrical about how proud we were to be there representing Australia, how much we admired the elite sudoku puzzlers and how much we hoped to learn by competing against the world's best. He was a magnificent ambassador and proved a tough act to follow.

In the lead-up to the tournament, we watched with interest as different countries confirmed their attendance. Each could send a maximum of four players. These four would compete as individuals and then the best three would combine their skills for the team event. If a country didn't have enough participants to make up a team, they would only be represented in the individual part of the competition.

In all, thirty nations were represented, with twenty sending enough to also compete in the team event.

Luxembourg was sending only one competitor, a female by the name of Claudine Thiry. Now, I'm not saying we went to India to try to score anywhere other than the tournament. But we were realists. We'd all heard the stories about the athletes in the Olympic village and we were at a world championship. We were only human, at the peak of our powers, and we all had needs. Let's just say that if Miss Luxembourg was lonely, we'd take her under our wing and, if nothing else, give her four handsome guys – Australian players no less – to hang out with.

We'd built the moment up from the time we saw Luxembourg's intention. So when the speeches finished, we put the plan into action. She was standing by herself and we seized our opportunity. We pumped up Skiffo and sent him over. He introduced himself.

'Hi. I'm Mark Skiffington. Captain of Australia.'

We thought we knew women. We thought for sure she'd go weak at the knees, stare at the crest on his blazer and be unable to contain herself. We were wrong. She just looked at him, proffered a polite smile and walked away.

In the short opening speech, we were all instructed to make our way to the main hall at about 9.30pm for the match-day briefing. My experience in the iron man competition should have been enough to convince me it was one meeting we should attend, but we decided against it. We weren't being arrogant. We just didn't think we'd learn anything that we couldn't find out the next morning.

Plus, Sandy and Hamish were busy. They'd convinced Ishant Sharma and his mate to hand over their guitars and were in the middle of a Kingfisher-fuelled version of the Jimi Hendrix classic 'Hey Joe'.

By the time the Sutherland brothers finished their one-song set, the place was empty; all the other competitors had gone to the briefing. While their night was winding down, ours was about to head in exactly the opposite direction.

When Marty Roebuck gave me one of his Wallaby jerseys, I tried to imagine what it must have been like for him to receive it in the first place. To sit in the dressing room before his first test and have someone present him with his own Australian jersey. A jersey he would wear when he ran out onto the field to play for Australia. But I couldn't imagine it. It was like me trying to imagine what it must be like to be Bono from U2, performing in front of 200,000 screaming fans. Or trying to imagine what it must be like to wake up next to Jennifer Aniston.

Mitch Hardy was a winger with the Gordon Rugby Club in Sydney before becoming an inaugural member of the ACT Brumbies when they joined the Super 12 competition in 1996. He went on to play for the Wallabies the following year.

His test debut against France in Sydney was something you could only dream about. He came on as a replacement in the fifty-ninth minute for Stephen Larkham, who left the field to get treatment for a facial injury. With his first touch of the ball, Mitch scored a try. With his second touch a few moments later, he scored another. He returned to the bench at the 71-minute mark when Larkham returned to the field. In the space of just twelve minutes, debutante Mitch Hardy scored two test tries, broke a 15–15 deadlock and set up Australia's 29–15 win.

It seemed that it was a night that couldn't get any better for him. But, only a few hours earlier, it had been a night that couldn't get much worse.

Like all players in his position, Mitch couldn't wait to get his hands on his very own Wallaby jersey. He'd been named in a team alongside some of Australian rugby's all-time greats – John Eales, George Gregan, Larkham, Jason Little and Tim Horan.

He sat in the dressing room, feeling a mixture of nerves and excitement. Then, the moment every young rugby player dreams of – the presentation of the jersey. These days, ex-Wallabies are given the honour of handing them out to the players. That night, it was being done by the coach, Greg Smith.

Smith worked his way through the team and came to Mitch. He addressed the young winger but not with the confidence-building rev-up you'd expect. Smith handed over the jersey and said that while he thought Mitch was a good club player, he hadn't thought he'd make it to this level.

Cop that.

It later came out that Smith was quite ill at the time. His behaviour became more erratic and in 1998 and 2001 he had emergency surgery for a brain tumour. Sadly, he passed away in September 2002, aged fifty-two.

We'd never be in a position to be presented with a Wallaby jersey but we would be receiving our Australian sudoku playing kit, which in our minds, was every bit as special. We headed back to our rooms and slipped into

A sight that would have filled the opposition with fear. Me before a game for the St Michael's Meadowbank Under 8s rugby league team.

My first taste of representative rugby and my first introduction to the great gear you get. Here with my Eastwood teammates in the Sydney Under 16 junior rugby team, I'm the awkward-looking one in the middle.

More false hope. Here I am with the Bryan Palmer Shield for being the 'Most Outstanding Colt'. Richard Harry was the runner-up. He went on to play 37 tests for Australia and win the Rugby World Cup in 1999. I didn't.

The Fibros versus the Silvertails. The Southwest Zone Under 18 team before our clash with the Northern Zone. I'm third from the left in the front row. My paddling partner, Bernard Walsh, is third from the left up the back.

Somewhere in Taiwan during the NSW Colleges tour of 1986. That's me, up the back, third from the left. The fullback in our side was Andrew Leeds, who became the Wallaby fullback later that same year.

The UWA 1st XV in 1992. I'm front row, third from the right. Skiffo is middle row, second from the right. My second-row partner, John Welborn (who's not in this photo), went on to become WA's first home-grown Wallaby, playing six tests.

With former Wallaby fullback Marty Roebuck and 'Bill', the name given to the William Webb Ellis Trophy by the Australians when they won the 1991 Rugby World Cup.

A change of sport but similar results. My first-ever iron-man race was a disaster and pretty much set the tone for my entire career. I'm third from the right.

Caddying for Steve Porch in 40-degree heat during the Heineken golf tournament at the Vines in Perth was great, but tough work. A cold towel is around my neck and I'm already struggling to keep up.

Left to right: Skiffo, Bayden the cameraman, Hamish and Sandy at Sam's Beach Shack before the official presentation of our playing kit.

Me, looking incredibly focused and totally switched on, at the airport with Matt and Ben. Like Shane Warne's kids and John Eales's kids, my boys can now say their dad played for Australia.

Looking proud at the opening ceremony of the Third World Sudoku Championship – the first official function in our Number 1s. Our blazers are a replica of the ones worn by the 1936 Olympic team.

The official team photo of the Members Equity Numbats Australian Sudoku Team.

Hamish and Sandy Sutherland, the first brothers since Steve and Mark Waugh to tour the subcontinent as part of an Australian team at an elite level.

It was 39 degrees but we refused to loosen our ties or remove our blazers at the opening dinner.

Looking immaculate but nervous before playing our first game in the green and gold.

The Australians in trouble during Round One of the teams event, with just two minutes and 50 seconds left on the clock. Each member had to complete one puzzle before progressing to the team table. We didn't make it.

70	LI Yiting	Korea (I)	70
70	Jean-Christophe Novelli	China	
70	Blanka Lehotska	France	
70	Martin Kollar	Slovakia	30
74	György István	Slovakia (I)	
75	Laura Tarchetti	Hungary (I)	
76	Sandy Sutherland	Italy	30
76	WANG Hongli	Australia	
76	Mariel Alexis Dee	China (I)	
79	G.M.Tanimul Ahsan	Philippines	
79	Henning Kalsgaard Poulsen	Bangladesh	30
81	Joëlle Rasneur	Denmark (I)	30
82	WU Kong-Jan	Belgium	
83	Hamish Sutherland	Chinese Taipei (I)	
83	Mick Colliss	Australia	
83	WANG Jia-Yao	Australia (I)	
83	Christof Bruetsch	Chinese Taipei (I)	
87	SK. A. S. M. Monirul Islam	Switzerland (I)	
87	Pierdante Lanzavecchia	Bangladesh	0
87	Simon Anthony	Italy	0
		United Kingdom (I)	0

The only score sheet that ever mattered. The rankings from the Third World Sudoku Championship after Round One.

Sandy, Skiffo and Hamish off to a flyer in Round Two of the teams event.

The Americans in action. That's our mate Wei-Hwa Huang on the left, with reigning world champion Thomas Snyder on the right. They beat us in the competition but our uniforms were better.

Hamish Sutherland, playing for Australia.

We found it highly amusing to be eating at an Indian restaurant in India. From left to right at the Delhi Darbar in Panaji: Sandy, Skiffo, Hamish, me and Bayden.

What puzzlers are wearing this summer.

Flashbacks to Year 12 during the Third World Sudoku Championships. The lady in blue and the guy in green couldn't believe their luck when Thomas Snyder sat down between them.

The top four competitors slug it out in the final. Their puzzles were broadcast on the big screen so we could monitor their progress.

Officially the best sudoku players in the world. From left to right: Jakub Ondrousek (Czech Republic) finished third; Thomas Snyder (USA) retained his world crown; and Yuhei Kusui (Japan) took home silver. Snyder pipped me by a mere 2680 points.

It's not every day you get to hang out with a world champion. The Australian team with Thomas Snyder from the USA.

One of the many fishing boats on the River Sal in Goa. The crew of 28 spend two weeks at sea and sleep anywhere on the deck where there aren't fish. It's a tough way to earn a dollar.

Bayden, me and Sandy during our boat cruise on the River Sal. Sandy wanted to book the boat for the following day so he could go 'skurfing down the Mekong' but his bottom wouldn't let him.

The Sudokumentary was like an Australian representative's reunion. From left to right: Skiffo (Numbat), Hamish (Numbat), Andy Taylor (Olympian) John Welborn (Wallaby), Cut-Out Sandy (Numbat), me (Numbat), Mitch Hardy (Wallaby), Tim Neesham (Triple Olympian), Sharan Wheelock (World Cup Gold Medallist and my wife). *Courtesy of the Community Newspaper Group.*

Cut-Out Sandy attracted many luminaries, including Damian O'Donnell, the ballboy for the Eastern Suburbs Roosters when they beat St George 38–0 in the 1975 rugby league grand final.

Australia's most-capped and highest-ever ranked international sudoku players. From left to right: Sandy Sutherland, Mark Skiffington, Mick Colliss and Hamish Sutherland.

something a little more comfortable – our team singlets and board shorts – before meeting at Sam's Beach Shack for the official presentation. It wasn't the most imposing structure but was our equivalent of a Twickenham, Cardiff Arms Park or Lansdowne Road.

Our playing kit was magnificent. Green and gold playing shirt with matching shorts and a pair of thongs, also green and gold, with 'AUS' printed on the top. The shirt and shorts were both embroidered with the Australian crest on the right hand side and the logo of our naming rights sponsor, Members Equity Bank, on the left.

Before we left, I had organised a keepsake in the form of a spare blazer pocket, which had been embroidered and framed. Each had a personalised plaque attached, which in Skiffo's case read, 'Presented to Mark Skiffington by the World Puzzle Federation – Australia, in recognition of your selection in the National Sudoku Team'.

I made a short speech expressing my pride in the moment and how much I was looking forward to playing the next day. Then I handed out the playing kit and memento to each member of the Australian team. There were handshakes and beers all round as we toasted our future success.

We must have projected a certain aura because we were approached by a couple of English tourists who wanted to know which Australian team we were. We puffed out our chests and proclaimed proudly, 'The sudoku team.' That was good enough for them. They stayed around, had their photo taken with us and shouted us some beers.

In the corner opposite us was a once-in-a-generation opportunity for the skipper. In fact, a once-in-a-three-generation opportunity. A very attractive daughter, her equally attractive mother and her surprisingly attractive grandmother were having a few drinks and strutting their stuff on the dance floor. It didn't take much convincing to get Skiffo up.

'Hello, ladies, I'm Mark Skiffington, captain of Australia.'

He had a couple of dances but didn't make much progress with any of the age groups. When you're a long way from home and your bearings are slightly off, you tend to lose your way a bit. That's why it's always good to get back to basics. In our case, we remembered a rule that had kept us out of trouble in the past and would keep us out of trouble now.

Big game, early night.

We'd come too far to waste the opportunity. It's not every day you wake up knowing you'll be representing your country in a World Championship.

CHAPTER 21
Playing for Australia

On the days I played rugby, I'd get really nervous and my mood would change significantly. I didn't like talking, I just liked keeping to myself. I had a strict routine and followed it to the letter, right down to the pieces of cloth I'd use to clean my boots. I'd hate to think what I would have been like if I had ever played at a decent level.

Now, waking up on the morning of my first game for Australia, I only had my rugby preparation for reference. I was noticeably quiet and decided to head down to the pool for a light swim. I jumped in but the result was not what I expected. The water felt exactly the same temperature as the air outside. So much for a refreshing start. I had a light breakfast and eyed off the opposition, who were busy with some last minute practice while they ate.

Sandy, Skiffo and Hamish wandered down shortly after, and my heart skipped a beat when I saw them arrive in their Australian playing kit. They looked magnificent.

Because we missed the briefing, we had no idea how the day would run, so Skiffo headed off to the main hall, the venue for the competition, to get some answers. While he was there, he bumped into Wei-Hwa Huang from the American team. It was a tense moment. We knew what he thought of us and we knew what we thought of him. It was like the captains of Manly and Wests bumping into each other in the foyer of that Melbourne hotel. While he was there, Skiffo picked up our competitor ID tags, which featured our names printed above the Australian flag.

I was still in my board shorts so headed back to my room to pad up. In a way, I was glad to be on my own.

I pulled out my Australian top and thought back to that day when I tried on Marty Roebuck's Wallaby jersey. I had promised myself that the next Australian top I wore would be my own and there I was, putting it on. It was a magical feeling.

You could actually sense the excitement outside the hall, where eighty-nine competitors from thirty different countries had gathered. My stomach was churning with nerves. I tried to relax. Told myself it wasn't life or death. But, deep down, I knew it was far more important than that.

I returned from doing yet another wee. I was wasting a lot of energy. Skiffo could sense it and pulled us aside. He told us to 'take a knee', so we gathered in a tight circle and crouched down.

We needed something special before the tournament began and the Australian skipper was about to deliver it.

He reminded us about our days playing rugby together and how much we would all have loved to have played for the Wallabies. He reminded us how lucky we were to have been given this opportunity to wear the green and gold and represent Australia. He remained calm but the intensity started to build. He then addressed us individually, starting with me.

'Mick,' he said. 'Forget the hard puzzles. Go straight for the classic sudoku. You just worry about getting off the mark. If you get five points for Australia here, you'll build on that. Remember, forget the rows and columns. Look after the boxes. Hamish, I think twenty-five or even thirty points is gettable for you. Start with the classic, then look for one of the harder ones. You can do it. Sandy, this is your time to step up. Your time to shine. Forget these other wankers. They all think we can't play. Get in there and show them we can.'

I'm sure the other puzzlers thought we were mad. We were in a huddle, getting all fired up. Snorting and grunting things like 'Come on' and 'Let's do this'. We were ready to run through a brick wall. It was the perfect build-up to a game of rugby. Except we were about to play a game of sudoku.

As I walked towards the double doors leading into the competition room, I felt like Billy Moore heading down the tunnel at Lang Park before Game One of the 1995 rugby league State of Origin series. Only, instead of shouting 'QUEENSLANDER!', I wanted to yell 'AUSTRALIAN!'. I told myself I was ready. Told myself I'd done all I could. That it was my time. I took a few deep breaths and walked in.

The room itself looked like it was about to host a high school exam. I got flashbacks to Year 12. There were fifty tables of two, with a large projector screen in front of the stage. On the screen were the words 'Time's Up', a simple message that would later become both an enemy and a friend.

I reserved two tables in the back left-hand corner. This was a source of much amusement to the hardened puzzlers, who were quick to point out that you couldn't sit next to one of your own team members. I don't know why. There would be no benefit in trying to cheat off each other.

A quick reshuffle saw me seated next to a German competitor. Hamish was on the table to my left. Sandy was on the table in front of me and Skiffo was one in front of Sandy.

One of the Belgian team members couldn't believe his luck when Thomas Snyder, the reigning world champion, sat down next to him. This was puzzling's equivalent of being paired with Tiger Woods at the British Open. There was a constant flash of cameras aimed at Snyder, who calmly took it all in his stride.

The first day of competition was made up of seven rounds lasting forty-five minutes each. Each round consisted of approximately twelve puzzles and the puzzles themselves were either classic sudoku – like the ones you see in the daily paper – or harder variations. The latter look nothing like the classics, but adhere to the same basic principles of having nine rows and columns in which no number can be repeated.

Each puzzle was worth a certain number of points, ranging from five to seventy-five, depending on the degree of difficulty.

The aim of each round was to complete as many puzzles as you could, and therefore score as many points as you could, in the allotted time.

To add to the confusion, the competition itself had two distinct divisions running concurrently. While the points scored for doing the classic sudoku puzzles went towards your overall total, they were also totalled separately. So, at the end of the tournament, there would be an overall

World Sudoku Champion and a World Classic Sudoku Champion.

The good puzzlers went for maximum points first, then worked their way backwards. The title of overall champion was the most coveted. Winning the Classic Sudoku title was like being named the leading try scorer. It's nice, but you still want to get your hands on the main prize.

At the end of the seven rounds, the top eight competitors would go into a sudden death quarter- and semifinal before the winner was decided.

As I sat there in the great hall at the Holiday Inn, wearing my green and gold Australian shirt, shorts, thongs and cap, about to compete in my first-ever world championship, I started to feel really nervous. It was all about to happen. Then I thought of the great Keith Miller, a former Australian cricketer, who fought as a pilot in World War II. When asked how he coped with the pressure of playing international cricket, he famously replied, 'There is no pressure in cricket. Pressure is a Messerschmitt up your arse.' That calmed me down. I looked at the German next to me and wondered if he'd find Miller's anecdote as funny as I did.

When all the competitors were seated, helpers wearing black polo shirts began handing out the puzzles, which were contained in a simple photocopied booklet. The booklet was placed face-down on the table in front of us. Spectators were lined up against the wall on either side, and also down the back. It must have been a record crowd for a World Sudoku Championship.

My wedding day went way too fast. I wasn't about to make the same mistake here. When I received my puzzle booklet, I took the time to sit back and soak it all in. I looked across the room and saw competitors with 'China' emblazoned across their backs. I saw Team Germany. And Estonia. I looked at Sandy, Mark and Hamish. I smiled when I saw the word 'Australia' proudly displayed across the broad shoulders of our nation's finest sudoku players.

The more experienced puzzlers had brought their own pencil cases and proceeded to pull out their lucky erasers and pencils, some in different colours. I assumed choosing between an HB and a 2B pencil was like choosing between 18- and 21-millimetre studs. At this level, the little things can make a big difference.

I picked up my complimentary freshly sharpened pencil and made a mental note to take it with me at the end of the day.

The screen had 45:00 projected onto it. We were told that this was the countdown clock. I told myself this was the scoreboard at Suncorp Stadium. The spectators were asked to be quiet. A hush fell over the competitors. It was like that moment before the first ball of a test match is bowled, that moment before kick-off in the World Cup final and that moment before the gates fly back at Flemington on that first Tuesday in November, all rolled into one.

The room was deadly silent. I could actually hear my heart beating. Then, the organiser made the announcement we'd been waiting so long to hear.

'You may start.'

I said to myself, 'I'm playing for Australia.'

The eyes began to water. I was away.

CHAPTER 22

World ranking

All that pent-up aggression from Skiffo's rousing pre-match address had to be directed somewhere and my Round One puzzle booklet became the target. I had no idea what to expect when I flipped it over. I turned to the first page and quickly replaced my aggression with fear. I had known there would be variations of the classic puzzle but these were unrecognisable. Trio Sudoku, Consecutive Sudoku, Extra Region Soduku, Quad Max, Group Sum, Non-Consecutive, Irregular, Diagonal. The list went on. And I didn't know how to start any of them.

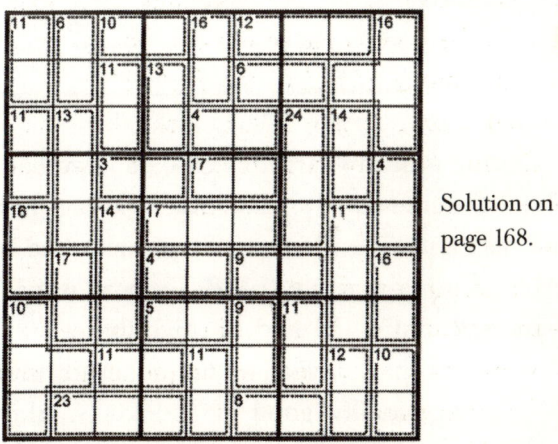

Solution on page 168.

I spotted one called Sum Sudoku and read the rules. 'The sum of the digits within each dotted subarea equals the number given in the top left-hand corner of that subarea.'

Right.

I turned the page and spotted Sudoku XV. It wasn't getting any better.

'All the adjacent cell pairs (sharing an edge) with two digits summing to 5 are marked by V, while those summing to 10 are marked by X.'

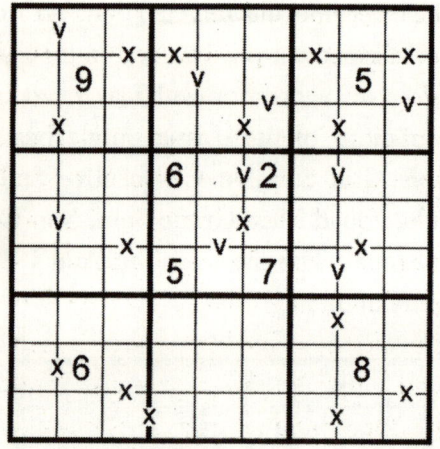

Solution on page 168.

During a third-year phys ed exam, we had a question about the menstrual cycle. One of the guys in my class put his hand up and asked if the males had to answer it. His reasoning was that the girls had an unfair advantage. I guessed asking if I had to solve these, on the grounds that every other player had an unfair advantage because they were actually good at sudoku, would have been fruitless.

I came to the conclusion that I'd be handing in a blank sheet. Great, if I was a soccer goalkeeper. Not so great when the whole aim of the competition was to fill in a series of forms.

With my heart rate at a panic-induced 200 beats per minute, I finally located the classic sudoku puzzle. I felt like I'd found a friend in a room full of strangers. When I finally began, I was focused and determined. And struggling.

Every time I looked up at the screen, another ten minutes had gone. I was beginning to think that Keith Miller might have re-evaluated his thoughts on pressure if he had attempted a puzzle at the World Sudoku Championship.

I stayed positive, though. Like John Eales, I thought about all those spectators who wished it was them sitting there, playing for their country. And slowly, it started coming together. I was finding numbers, getting into a rhythm and filling in the blanks. All the advice from the skipper came flooding back. All those years of training kicked in and I didn't think, I just did. I placed the last number with four minutes twelve seconds remaining on the clock. I quickly scanned the puzzle to make sure I hadn't doubled up any numbers. I hadn't. I'd done it. And I was jubilant.

I made a fist and pumped it under the desk. I looked for Bayden and gave him the thumbs up.

I felt like Tanzanian runner John Akhwari at the 1968 Mexico City Olympics. He started the marathon with all the other runners but finished it alone, more than an hour after the winner. There were only a few spectators remaining in the stands when Akhwari entered the stadium, bandaged and bloody, to cross the finish line.

When asked by a reporter why he hadn't just quit, he answered, 'My country did not send me to Mexico City to start the race. They sent me here to finish.'

That was me. It had taken me nearly the whole time and what I had done was only worth five points, but I'd finished a puzzle for Australia.

I watched the clock count down and when the words 'Time's Up' appeared on screen, we all put our pencils down. The helpers quickly moved through the room, collecting the booklets for marking. The person marking mine must've been pretty happy – it wouldn't have taken them very long.

Once all the booklets had been collected, we were allowed to take a fifteen-minute break before Round Two began.

Anyone who says sudoku is just a game is kidding themselves. Sandy, Skiffo, Hamish and I had been involved in some fantastic rugby matches that have only been decided in the last second. But I doubt we'd ever been as animated as we were after Round One. We knew we were out of our depth, but we had actually finished a world championship-standard puzzle. Against all odds, we actually felt like we belonged. We were not just immersed in the world of international puzzling, we were embracing it.

We headed back in for Round Two, high on confidence and with the pressure of finishing a puzzle now well behind us. With early runs on the board, we focused on the task of scoring points, which counted towards not only our individual scores but also our team score. While we each managed to repeat our earlier heroics and finish at least one puzzle in both Rounds Two and Three, our lack of match fitness started to show, which was a real concern at such an early stage.

Each round was forty-five minutes. That's forty-five minutes of pure concentration. To sit down and work your brain that hard for that long is a very difficult thing, especially when you're not used to it. The fifteen-minute break between each round was a godsend.

If Thomas Snyder was the Tiger Woods of puzzling, team mate Wei-Hwa Huang was the Greg Matthews.

Matthews, the spinner from New South Wales, played a key role for Australia in the famous tied test against India in Madras in 1986. This was the game where a dangerously dehydrated Dean Jones, a Victorian, told his batting partner, captain Allan Border, that he wanted to leave the field midway through the first innings. He'd been vomiting because of the heat and humidity, and was obviously unwell. With Greg Ritchie next man in, Border replied (among other things), 'You can go off – we'll get a real Aussie man out here. A Queenslander.'

Jones batted on and finished with a career-defining 220 from 330 balls. After the completion of his marathon innings he had to be treated in hospital for heat exhaustion.

When it was Australia's turn to bowl, the Indians were all out for 397, with Matthews taking 5 for 103. Despite the oppressive heat, Matthews wore a jumper for the entire time. It was his way of telling the Indians there was nothing they could dish out that Australia couldn't take. It was psychological warfare at its very best.

After 135 minutes of puzzling, our brains were cooked and we couldn't think straight. We needed the scheduled breaks to clear our heads. Other players were obviously feeling the same way. But not Huang. Instead of relaxing during the fifteen minutes, he sat on the steps directly outside the main hall, in full view of everyone, and did puzzles. Snyder used a different method to show that he was completely in control. He pulled out a puzzle and started doing it up against the wall. He was showboating. Almost as soon as he started, he was surrounded by a group of about twenty people, all jostling for a position and taking photos of the great man in action. The Rock Star was on fire.

If I needed any reminding that this was a world championship and the title of World Champion was on the line, I got it at the end of Round Four. People had won National Titles to be here and paid good money to travel to India. Results were important. When the scores for Round One were posted on a notice board outside the main entrance, word spread quickly and puzzlers flocked from everywhere. They were like hungry seagulls fighting over a chip.

We were under no illusions and started our search from the bottom. No one was more surprised than me to discover we were not there.

In eighty-ninth place was Simon Anthony from the United Kingdom. In eighty-eighth, Pierdante Lanzavecchia from Italy. In eighty-seventh, it was SK.A.S.M Monrul Islam from Bangladesh, and eighty-sixth was Christof Bruetch from Switzerland. In eighty-fifth place was Jia-Yao Wang from Chinese Taipei. And in eighty-fourth place was Mick Colliss from Australia. Unbelievable. I'd taken an international scalp. Hell, this was no time for modesty. I'd taken FIVE international scalps. Count 'em! This was better than anything I could have possibly imagined. Hamish was level with me, Sandy was in seventy-sixth position and Skiffo was in sixty-eighth, after one of the great captain's knocks.

To a man, we felt as though we had proved ourselves on the world stage. Skiffo's shot at the world title was back on. We were no longer the well-dressed jokes of the competition. We were genuine contenders.

Our tactic of going for the easy puzzles paid off. Hamish and I picked up five points as planned. The people below us must have gone for the big points, stuffed up and run out of time. They ended up with the duck egg.

If the tournament had finished then and there I wouldn't have complained. I'd already peaked and knew it would be all downhill from there for me, as far as rankings were concerned.

The rest of the day was difficult, but I had expected nothing less. No one said representing Australia in a world championship would be easy. My personal highlight occurred in Round Four, when I completed a classic sudoku puzzle in less than nine minutes. Apparently, I was supposed to use some of the numbers from that puzzle as clues for solving the next one, but I didn't know which, so I spent the next thirty-six minutes cursing myself for missing the briefing. When 'Time's Up' flashed onto the screen, I felt as though I'd let Australia down. If only I'd had more time.

Confidence is a wonderful thing. According to the late rugby league supercoach Jack Gibson, 'That's what puts the ball in the hole.' After my Round Four heroics, the success started to go to my head. In fact, we all started getting a bit cocky.

I was sitting on thirty points. Hamish was on twenty-five. Sandy had 140 against his name and Skiffo, a Dean Jones-esque 220. Before we knew it, we started talking ourselves up. Our focus switched from external to internal. It was no longer Australia versus the world. We were more concerned with beating each other. It was mate versus mate. And it was ugly.

You can't put a price on a good captain – they see things others can't. Skiffo knew that the tactics of going for the harder puzzles just to move up the national rankings was wrong and selfish. He pulled us aside and asked us what we were thinking. Why was it suddenly more important for me to beat Hamish, or for Sandy to beat Skiffo, than it was for all of us to concentrate on beating someone from Belarus or Poland? Once again, he was right. I almost felt embarrassed by my behaviour.

Round Five was a solid one for the Numbats. I managed to add ten points to my tally by completing another classic sudoku, while the Sutherland brothers finished two puzzles to register twenty-five points each. The skipper tried a tougher puzzle and nailed it to score fifty-five points for his country. Things were looking up.

The penultimate round was high on quality if not quantity. Hamish, Sandy and I each finished a classic puzzle worth twenty-five points. Skiffo knocked off two for a total of sixty points.

We decided to go all out in Round Seven. Have a real crack. All or nothing. Unfortunately, it was the latter. Even the so-called easiest puzzle was beyond the four of us. I kept looking at the screen, wishing those two simple words would appear and put me out of my misery.

At least the spare time I had gave me a chance to watch some of the better competitors in action. I noticed that Huang did puzzles with a pencil in both hands. He spun them like they were nunchakas, switching from the lead point to the eraser on the other end as he worked his way through. He was like a ninja and the pencils were his weapons. If he had a third hand, I'm sure he'd find a use for that too. Other puzzlers started with a lead pencil, then switched to a different colour when they made a calculated guess. If they got it wrong, this made it easy for them to see where they started guessing and backtrack. It was fascinating stuff.

When the results of the overall competition were published at the end of the home and away rounds, we held our heads high. We'd missed out on the play-offs, but we'd made a stunning debut. Skiffo maintained his wonderful form and finished in eighty-third place with 335 points. Sandy came a respectable eighty-fifth with 190 points, and Hamish a competitive eighty-eighth with seventy-five points.

My total of sixty-five points dropped me from the nosebleed heights of eighty-fourth to eighty-ninth. But I was okay with that. After all, it wasn't just any old eighty-ninth. It was eighty-ninth in the world.

More surprising were the results from the Classic Sudoku division.

Skiffo was in seventy-seventh place, Sandy in eighty-first, Hamish was in eighty-seventh and I was in eighty-eighth.

Jia-Yao Wang from Chinese Taipei was set to become the answer to perhaps the greatest trivia-night question of all time. It will be up there with 'Which Australian batsman made the record books for being given out for handling the ball whilst at the non-striker's end during a test match in 1979?', and 'Who chipped in from 140 feet to beat Greg Norman at the second play-off hole at the 1987 Masters in Augusta?': 'Who did Mick Colliss beat in the classic division of the 3rd World Sudoku Championships?'

In the team competition, Australia was sitting in twentieth place out of twenty with a total of 385 points. We decided that was cause for celebration because we were only 210 points behind Bangladesh. We knew that nineteenth in the world was well within our grasp.

It had been a great day.

CHAPTER 23

Come on, Australia

Lawrence Rowe was just another nervous young cricketer when he made his test debut for the West Indies against New Zealand in Kingston, Jamaica, in 1972. A few days later, his name was etched in history, having scored 214 in the first innings and 100 not out in the second.

While my first game for my country wasn't quite as impressive, it was still a very significant occasion. It wasn't every day you made your debut for the mighty Members Equity Numbats Australian Sudoku Team.

When the day's play ended we were still on a high, so we grabbed the plastic cricket bat and rubber ball and made our way to the beach in front of our hotel. We were pleasantly surprised to see a number of participants from the other teams heading in the same direction, and had visions of holding an impromptu international beach cricket tournament that would last well into the night.

We had a quick swim as part of our post-game recovery, then set up on the water's edge, using the thin film of water from each retreating wave as the pitch. It was lightning-fast so we set a deep first slip and did our best to take each other's heads off with some short-pitched deliveries that rose sharply. When we checked on the progress of our rivals, we were happy with the numbers but disappointed with their lack of enthusiasm for the game. They weren't even watching. They were sitting on sun lounges doing puzzles.

Before too long, the hot Indian conditions took their toll and we adjourned to Sam's Beach Shack for an extended drinks break, which flowed seamlessly into tea before stumps were called at around 11pm.

The media hype we created before we left Australia continued while we were in India, with radio stations across the country requesting a progress report during the competition. I was happy to oblige but the different time zones meant waking to give interviews at 1am, 2am, 3.30am and 5.30am. I wasn't involved in the competition the following day, so it was only fair that I was the one with the disrupted sleep.

Day two of the World Sudoku Championship was the team part of the competition. On the starter's orders, three representatives from each country had to complete four individual puzzles before making their way to their designated team table. Each individual puzzle contained clues that would help solve the team puzzle, the idea being that everyone worked together to try to get it finished within the time limit. While points were awarded for each individual puzzle completed, the big scores didn't start rolling in until everyone got together.

I was very excited by the prospect of the team event. I'd had the pleasure of playing for Australia and now I was about to watch the Australian team in action. When all the competitors had taken their seats and the room once again fell quiet in anticipation, I found myself yelling, 'Come on, Australia!' It felt like a thousand eyes were suddenly cast in my direction. Some puzzlers appeared shocked by my boorish behaviour. Others, I'm sure, wished their supporters were as vocal. It was the World Championship after all.

The Le Mans start didn't suit the Australian team, and Sandy, Skiffo and Hamish never made it to the group table. The best Skiffo had done in any one round on the first day was three puzzles, a new Australian record. Expecting everyone to finish four with enough time to work on a fifth was ambitious, to say the least.

The Australians had much better luck in the second round of the team event, mainly because they started at the team table, with all players working on the same puzzle from the beginning.

But while the change in format was better, the result wasn't.

As if the puzzles hadn't been hard enough, the final one was delivered in nine pieces. The first task was actually to construct the grid by arranging each individual block of nine in the correct order. Once that was done, you could start trying to solve it. It was a task that proved impossible for the combined brain power of the mighty Numbats and, like the great Don Bradman, we failed to trouble the scorers in our last innings for Australia.

When the final tallies were released, Australia hung on to twentieth position with a grand total of 750 points — another national record. It was a very pleasing result and only 9952 points behind the Czech Republic, who was crowned World Champion Team.

With our playing commitments over, it was time to settle back with a couple of six packs of warm Kingfisher and watch the big boys of sudoku in action.

The top eight individual competitors were lined up, two to a table, across the front of the hall. When they finished a puzzle on the first table, they jumped out of their seats and moved one table forward, where another puzzle was waiting. When they finished that puzzle, they moved to table three, completed a puzzle and then went to table four. The first four competitors to complete a puzzle at each of the four tables progressed to the final.

Two of the rounds from the previous day were classed as bonus rounds, which meant competitors would get a time advantage if they had finished all twelve puzzles in that particular round in less than forty-five minutes. These were the same rounds in which I had taken forty-one minutes to complete one simple classic sudoku. For every minute they finished ahead of time, they would get a thirty-second head start in the quarter-final.

The final eight positions were seeded, with Czech Jakub Ondrousek (2810 points) starting in lane one. Ondrousek had earned a three-minute head start over the USA's man-child Thomas Snyder (2745 points) in lane two. Interestingly, Ondrousek and I both finished this World Championship with a personal best next to our name.

The leap-frog format was a fantastic way to run a quarter-final because the normally sedate sudoku crowd showed signs of life for the first time in two days. There was audible cheering as they watched positions change and saw lower-ranked competitors move ahead of their more fancied rivals. Despite his head start, Ondrousek was clearly feeling the pressure, and it was Snyder, the man with the big game experience, who was first to move.

For forty-five minutes, competitors and spectators were on the edge of their seats, enthralled by a competition that was surprisingly exciting.

Third seed Yuhei Kusui from Japan flew through the third puzzle and overtook Snyder. He held his nerve to be first into the final, while the American cruised through in second place. Jakub Hrazdira from the Czech Republic became our favourite when he did a Kieren Perkins and made it through from lane eight.

David McNeill from the United Kingdom and Ondrousek were on their fourth and final puzzle when the countdown clock reached zero. Instead of playing extra time, the organisers worked on a countback rule and decided Ondrousek was the one to progress because of his higher seeding.

McNeill was devastated. We didn't care. England had broken our hearts when they beat Australia to win the Ashes in 2005. This was payback. I wished I could be the one handing out his boarding pass for his flight home. Then I'd really rub it in.

The excitement continued for the final, when the top four competitors were lined up on stage, facing the audience. Cameras were positioned above each competitor's desk and their puzzles projected onto a large screen behind them, allowing spectators to ride with them as they worked their way through. We have race-cam, helmet-cam and stump-cam. Puzzle-cam was a natural progression.

Speed was the key to victory. Every second you finish a puzzle ahead of your competitor was a second head start you got in the following round. It was amazing to see how quickly those elite players could complete a game of sudoku.

It was also good to see that they were human. In the third round, every competitor got more than three-quarters of the way through their puzzle before realising they'd made a mistake. It made for great viewing and the crowd let out a collective 'ooohhh' each time the best in the world were forced to reach for their rubbers, erase the whole thing and start again.

In recent years, active recovery has become the norm for footballers rested during games. It's not uncommon to see players riding stationary pushbikes on the sideline while they wait to return to the field.

Snyder followed the same principle during the final, doing Find-a-Word puzzles to keep his mind active in between rounds, much to the delight of his growing fan base.

When Marty Roebuck was playing in the 1991 Rugby World Cup held in England, I stayed awake until all hours so I could watch him play. He was a mate, striving to be a world champion. Staying up to watch was a given. Thomas Snyder was playing for the World Title. His team mate Wei-Hwa Huang was in the same hall. But was he watching? Cheering? Offering support? No. Huang was doing puzzles. He was one strange cat. At least he was wearing his shirt.

Snyder had taken a one-minute-fifty-eight-second lead into the fourth and final round. It was like giving Makybe Diva a three-length start in the Melbourne Cup. The reigning World Champion was just too talented and, despite a late challenge from Kusui, went on to win back-to-back titles. I waited for him to stand up and shout, 'Thomas Snyder, World Champion!', but instead he pulled out his Find-a-Word book and quietly continued while he waited for everyone else to finish. Kusui took the silver medal, Ondrousek was third and Hrazdira fourth.

The closing ceremony was extremely low key. There was no fanfare, no glitter falling from the ceiling, no fireworks. I thought at a World Championship – the pinnacle of sudoku puzzling – more would be made of the winners. Maybe that's not puzzling's style, but it should be. The WPF has a great opportunity to build on what they have. It should be an event that people go home talking about and are desperate to be part of.

We'd never really felt the love from the other competitors, which I thought was a bit strange. I'd thought there'd be more interaction. In most world championship events, there are the powerhouses and the minnows, and there was no doubt we were the minnows. Without putting them down, we were like Scotland in the ICC Cricket World Cup and Namibia in the Rugby World Cup. We'd been there to compete and learn from the best but had never managed to break into the inner circle and mix with the true superstars of the game. Although Thomas Snyder had come across and shown us how to do one of the puzzles we couldn't figure out from the team event. That had been cool. Like being shown how to surf by Kelly Slater.

We were confident that the final night was going to be a huge party but we were disappointed. Once again, we sat at the table marked Australia, ate the banquet and drank warm beer. Then the night went downhill. Maybe we were mentally drained. Maybe we had played our best games at Sam's Beach Shack. There was no game the following day, but we just couldn't fire a shot. By 10.30pm, we were all in bed.

We were officially elite puzzlers.

CHAPTER 24

Hard beds, soft stools

'Uh oh.'

These were the words that greeted me when Skiffo woke on the morning after the competition. He jumped out of bed and ran to the bathroom. Maybe it's a one-off. Maybe not. No sooner was he back on his bed than he was racing to the bathroom again. This routine continued for the entire day.

Hamish had caught an early flight back home, so Sandy, Bayden and I decided to take a look around and experience some of the local culture. We'd been so caught up in the competition, we'd almost forgotten we were in another part of the world.

As it turned out, our hotel was only about 100 metres away from the mighty River Sal, a large, busy waterway dotted with fishing villages that drains into the Arabian Sea. A number of the roadside shacks offered river cruises, so we made a booking and followed a narrow, winding dirt path down to the water.

The boat waiting for us was about thirty feet long, but it was no *Bertram*. Made of splintering fibreglass, it was narrow, with a row of plastic chairs down each side. There was no service on board, so we borrowed an Esky from the adjoining Fisherman's Wharf Bar and Grill, bought a dozen stubbies of Foster's and watched as the staff kindly chipped some ice out of their freezer to help keep our beers cold.

The trip down the river was one of the highlights of the tour. While Goa is a tourist area, life on the riverbanks is about as far removed from it as could be. We passed boats that had just returned from two weeks at sea, absolutely overloaded with fish. The crew of twenty-eight didn't have official sleeping quarters. Anywhere they could find a space was bed for the night. It's a tough way to earn a dollar.

Small communities appeared every couple of hundred metres. Women washed clothes in the river and children played happily amongst the rubbish piled up next to makeshift accommodation.

We saw men in hand-carved canoes sitting in the middle of the river fishing, and others walking along dragging nets. It was a simple existence and we felt privileged to see it in such an up-close and personal way.

Even though we were more than 3500 kilometres from Vietnam, cruising down the River Sal evoked memories of the film *Apocalypse Now*. Sandy took things to another level when he decided to book the boat again for the following morning. He had noticed an old windsurfer board back at the wharf and his grand plan involved 'skurfing down the Mekong' while the song 'Purple Haze' blasted from his iPod speakers.

With all our beer consumed, we were at a point where we thought that was one of the best ideas we'd ever heard.

A sober Skiffo, with buttocks tightly clenched, was waiting at the wharf to greet us when our cruise ended. He noticed a dead fish in the river, then watched as a plastic bag and a large piece of wood floated by. Needless to say, he didn't share our enthusiasm.

Knowledge can be a dangerous thing. Before I studied phys ed, if I had a sore shoulder, it was simply that – a sore shoulder. But with a degree under my belt, a sore shoulder became anything from a torn rotator cuff to a macrotrauma of the glenohumeral cavity. It was always far more serious.

When I woke the next day with a slight ache in my stomach to match the one in my head, I automatically thought the worst. I walked carefully to the bathroom and the result wasn't pretty. I returned to my bed then headed straight back to the bathroom for round two.

That's when I started to worry. Skiffo had spent the past twenty-four hours on the toilet. The only positive he could find in the whole scenario was that it hadn't been a travel day. Today *was* the travel day and I had the stomach cramps.

We rang Sandy and it took three calls before we got through. Each time he tried to answer the phone, he had to detour to the bathroom. There would be no skurfing the Mekong. While Sandy was in a worse state than I was, he remained relatively calm because his flight wasn't until the following day. However, fearful of lacking the necessary speed to make it to safety when the need arose, he bade us a hurried farewell.

If there was ever a time I needed to harness the power of my mind, this was it. The bus to Goa airport left in three hours, and I had a further eighteen hours of travel and transit ahead of me. Skiffo thought he'd turned the corner but dared not risk breaking wind. I was lying on one of the hardest, most uncomfortable beds I'd ever slept on but didn't dare risk standing for fear of the effects gravity may have on the contents of my bowel.

We both lay there like kittens, watching a movie on the Hallmark channel, counting down the hours and praying we'd dry up.

Every speed bump we hit in the Partridge Family bus was a challenge but we managed to maintain our dignity. Thankfully, my illness didn't seem to be getting any worse and Skiffo demonstrated the same levels of mental toughness that saw him finish the tournament as Australia's highest-ever ranked international sudoku player.

While we had almost expected to get some sort of diarrhoea, the thing we most wanted to avoid was malaria. A couple of days on the toilet was nothing compared with periodic fever, varying degrees of anaemia and splenic enlargement, and a range of syndromes resulting from the physiological and pathological involvement of certain organs, including the brain, liver and kidneys.

When we landed in Mumbai we were put on a shuttle bus to be transferred to the international terminal. The bus was full of mosquitoes. Hungry mosquitoes. It was a five-minute trip that seemed to last an hour. When we got off, we were covered in self-inflicted welts caused by preventative slapping.

We had six hours to kill at Mumbai airport, so decided to check in and head straight for the Qantas club. Nice idea in principle. There isn't a Qantas club in Mumbai. We were told we could go to a common lounge, so we tried that, only to be informed that we couldn't go in because our tickets were booked as Jet Airways. I tried to explain that it was a Qantas affiliate and our flight number was a

Qantas number, but the Andrew Symonds-hating lady on reception pointed out that our boarding passes were for Jet, not Qantas. She refused to budge.

Finally, we opened our wallets and offered to pay, and suddenly we were talking the same language. We got ourselves in, pulled up chairs in front of the TV, and spent the rest of our time in India watching New Zealander Brendan McCullum set a new world record, as he smashed an unbeaten 158 not out for the Kolkata Knightriders in the opening game of the IPL Twenty 20 competition.

Sitting in that crowded lounge at Mumbai airport, enjoying a complimentary room-temperature Kingfisher beer, gave me a chance to reflect on a journey that was, sadly, almost at its end.

It had taken me forty-two years but I could finally cross 'represent Australia' off my list of things to do. Against all odds, I'd competed for my country. I'd worn the green and gold with pride alongside my mates. I'd experienced the joy of having my dream come true. I'd travelled to India, 'the final frontier', as former Australian cricket captain Steve Waugh had called it. I owned an Australian blazer, an Australian playing kit and an assortment of other items, all embroidered with our coat of arms. I had enough memories to last a lifetime and a future in which I would be able to sit my grandchildren on my knee and regale them with stories about the time I played for Australia.

I didn't cover myself in glory but I had a go. And, to me, that's what being Australian is all about.

CHAPTER 25

The wrap-up

Six months after our triumphant return to Australian shores, I'm still hoping we'll be honoured with a ticker tape parade and I've bought a new suit to wear when I dine at The Lodge with our prime minister. All I need is an invitation.

Skiffo is discovering that fame comes at a price and he's constantly being challenged by sudoku fans wanting to test themselves against the Australian captain. He says he can appreciate what it must be like for someone like Danny Green, the former world-champion boxer, who has every second drunk he meets wanting to take him on. Like Skiffo says, if you're at a party with Olympic 100-metre gold medallist Usain Bolt, you don't ask him to go down to the park for a race. Sure, come up, say g'day, grab an autograph and a photo. No problem. But don't punish Skiffo for having a mind like a steel trap. Let him live a normal life.

Hamish returned to teaching and has continued to improve his sudoku skills. He was bitten by the bug and, while he's not obsessed, he is a genuine fan. He's thinking about introducing sudoku into the school curriculum in the hope of unearthing the next Thomas Snyder. Hamish has made it clear that when he retires from playing, he wants to coach so he can stay closely involved in the game he loves.

Sandy's career mirrored that of Bob Egerton, the former Wallaby winger from Sydney University, who burst on to the international representative scene in 1991. It was short but sweet. Like Sandy, Bob played nine games for Australia. He made his test debut against Wales on 22 July and played his final game just thirteen weeks later, when he helped the Wallabies defeat England 12–6 in the Rugby World Cup final. While Sandy dabbles with the occasional puzzle when he's in transit, he has avoided the limelight. His brush with the glamorous world of international sudoku is now nothing more than a cherished memory.

Bayden, our cameraman, ended up with twenty-eight hours of footage. How he didn't end up in hospital from exhaustion is beyond me. I have never seen anyone work as hard as he did. He'd be with us at the bar till stumps, but the next morning be up, camera in tow, shooting elephants, scenery, or recording interviews with the stars of international sudoku, names like Ondrousek, McNeill, Huang and Snyder. Bayden is now back in Melbourne, shooting TV commercials, documentaries and short movies under the Findlay Films banner.

The director, Scott Baskett, and his producer, Michael Green, had the mammoth task of trying to edit the footage into something resembling entertainment. We didn't really give them a lot to work with, and sudoku isn't exactly an exciting spectator sport. However, they managed to do it.

We organised a special preview screening of *Colours by Numbers, the Sudokumentary* for friends and family. It was a good chance for Scott, Michael and Bayden to see how people would react to their months of toil. Their aim is to have it picked up by one of the networks or an international distributor. While they were hoping for a positive response, we were hoping we wouldn't embarrass ourselves, so it was a nervous time for everyone.

More than 200 people, all adhering to the dress code of 'black tie with a touch of green and gold', gathered in the main theatre at the University of Western Australia. The guest list was like a who's who of Australian sport. We had Olympians, World Cup gold medallists, Wallabies and a dual Hawaiian Iron Man. But the biggest cheer of the night was for a man who, like us, is intent on chasing a lifelong dream.

Graham Mason has recently been crowned the Western Australian State Monopoly Champion. He is an official state champion, having beat sixty other people – children and pensioners included – to claim the title. No one can take it away from him. Graham is about to head to Melbourne, where he'll contest the Australian Monopoly Championship. If he wins there, he'll wear the green and gold as Australia's representative at the World Monopoly Championship in Las Vegas. Graham said I inspired him. It's the greatest compliment I've ever received.

About the only person who wasn't there was Sandy. That surprised everyone. He had a meeting in Sweden and couldn't make it back. So we organised a lifesize corflute cut-out to be there in his place. By the end of the function, cut-out Sandy was far better behaved, more coherent and a much better conversationalist than the real thing would have been. Last we saw, cut-out Sandy was being taken away by one of the male guests.

The sudokumentary itself was fantastic. It kicked off with a rendition of 'Advance Australia Fair' so full of passion it made the hairs on the back of my neck stand up. Thankfully, the crowd loved every minute of the film and laughed in all the right places. There was even spontaneous applause when they saw the presentation of our playing kit at Sam's Beach Shack. It was amazing for us to look back on what we'd accomplished, to see the joy on our faces at the end of that first round. To hear Thomas Snyder say he admired the way we played as a team.

I remember asking Marty Roebuck what it feels like to sit down and watch a video of one of his test matches. To sit back and try to comprehend the significance of what he's achieved. To sit there and think 'That's me.' All he'd ever say was, 'Yeah. It's good.'

He's dead right.

While Sharan is happy that I've finally lived my dream, she thinks playing in one world championship is enough. She says I need to let it go. That there are better things we can spend our money on. I think it's because she wants to be the only person in our house who can say they went to two. It's hard enough for her to accept that she's no longer the only one with a framed Australian team uniform up on the wall. She still rolls her eyes whenever I leave the house in my Australian shorts, or when I threaten to introduce myself to a stranger sitting down doing a sudoku puzzle at one of our local cafés.

She thinks it's time I stepped aside and let a new generation of sudoku puzzlers experience the thrill of playing for their country. She reckons it would be great to see an Australian going head to head with Thomas Snyder for the world title. And it would be, too. I really hope someone picks up where we left off. Although I might have to establish an Australian Sudoku Hall of Fame while I can, and induct Hamish, Skiffo, Sandy and me, so our place in history can be guaranteed alongside the future greats.

My two boys, Matt and Ben, have been unaffected by my glory. They certainly haven't been targeted at school like the kids of other famous sports stars. And they certainly won't feel under any pressure to be as good as their old man. Not unless they start up a sudoku club. Which would be quite sad. Matt is actually quite good at the game and he's always quick to tell his friends that his dad was in the Australian team. Ben's not quite as enthusiastic about my role. While he thinks I'm good, he's quick to point out that I'm not as good as Matt Giteau.

As for me? Well, I've struggled. The transition from the world of international sudoku to normal society has been much harder than I thought. I can now sympathise with other elite athletes such as Ian Thorpe and Shane Gould. Deidre Anderson, a highly regarded transition specialist, worked with both of them and speaks often of the trauma retirement brings. Maybe I should give her a call.

The main problem is I feel like I've lost my identity. For so long, I was Mick Colliss, Vice-Captain of the Members Equity Numbats Australian Sudoku Team. So many of my conversations centred on the training, the tour, the performance. Now, I'm just Mick Colliss.

I'm still battling my demons. But it's a small price to pay.

Solutions to Sample Puzzles:

Puzzle from page 141.

¹¹8	⁶1	¹⁰4	6	¹⁶9	¹²2	3	7	¹⁶5
3	5	¹¹9	¹³8	7	4	⁶2	1	6
¹⁶6	¹³7	2	5	⁴1	3	²⁴9	¹⁸8	4
5	4	³1	2	¹⁷8	9	7	6	⁴³3
¹⁶9	2	¹⁴3	¹⁷7	4	6	8	¹⁵5	1
7	¹⁷8	6	⁴1	3	⁹5	4	2	¹⁶9
¹⁰1	9	5	⁵3	2	⁹8	⁵⁷6	4	7
2	3	¹⁷7	4	¹⁶6	1	5	¹²9	¹⁰8
4	²³6	8	9	5	⁸7	1	3	2

Puzzle from page 142.

1ᵛ4	2	7	5	8	3	9	6

(solution grid with operators)

1ᵛ4	2	7	5	8	3	9	6
6	9	8	3ᵛ2	1	7	5	4
7×3	5	9	6×4	8×2	1
9	5	7	6	3ᵛ2	1ᵛ4	8
3ᵛ2	4	8	1×9	6	7	5
8	1	6	5	4	7	2ᵛ3	9
5	8	3	4	7	6	9×1	2
4×6	1	2	9	3	5	8	7
2	7	9×1	8	5	4×6	3

Honour Roll

Name	Number of games for Australia	Points scored
Rechelle Hawkes	279	49
George Gregan	139	99
Sharan Wheelock	116	128
Stephen Larkham	102	135
David Campese	101	315
John Eales	86	173
Matt Burke	81	878
Michael Lynagh	72	911
Phil Kearns	67	34
Richard Harry	37	5
Wally Lewis	33	45
Andrew Johns	24	184
Marty Roebuck	23	115
Mark Skiffington	9	335
Sandy Sutherland	9	190
Hamish Sutherland	9	75
Rob Egerton	9	8
Mitch Hardy	8	10
Mick Colliss	7	65
John Welborn	6	0

Backword

I understand how lucky I am to have been given the honour of wearing the green and gold. It really is a privilege, and the memories I have of the time I played for Australia are ones I will always cherish. I grew up idolising some of our greatest athletes, and four of my favourites kindly agreed to share their thoughts as part of this book.

> *There would be very few kids in the country that believe one day they are going to represent Australia. Just playing first-grade football is seemingly regarded as the highest target achievable, and for those that achieve that, they are eternally grateful. Donning the famous green and gold is an experience that will never be forgotten, but it also creates another immediate challenge. To never let down those who have created the history and pride associated with the honour, nor those that support them.*
>
> Wally Lewis, rugby league immortal

> *It's the dream for a lot of Aussies to wear the green and gold and represent their country.*
>
> *I was lucky enough to do so and the pride and feeling of accomplishment is immense; one which never leaves you.*
>
> *Mick, Mark, Hamish and Sandy achieved it in the most unusual way — via SUDOKU.*

> *Aah! What the heck!*
> *Well done boys.*
>
> Dennis Lillee, Australian cricket legend

It is with great pride that I call myself Australian and it is with even greater pride that I can say that I have represented my country. To compete at the highest level and go up against the best in the world is one of the most satisfying experiences.

Rechelle Hawkes, triple Olympic gold medallist

I've always been a man of words. You may be able to tell by the fact that I am a commentator. I speak a lot of rubbish but you get that from people who like words. Give me an essay. Give me English, history, philosophy but don't give me numbers. Maths, statistics, algorithms are foreign, alien in fact. I failed quantitative methods three times at university before I had to go back to introduction to statistics. I'm more comfortable with words but at the end of the day that's all they are ... words.

Those who can do numbers, that understand the nuances of a quadratic equation, who can rise to the feats of binomial distributions. They are the ones I really respect. Archimedes, Euclid, Isaac Newton and Pythagoras. They are the real heroes. They were the ones that could sit down and complete a sudoku puzzle with ease. Like Eales jumping in a lineout, like Horan linking with Little, and like Steve Larkham dropping a field goal from 47 metres in a World Cup semifinal. They make it look easy.

Mick Colliss is in this league. His desire to represent Australia at something ... anything ... drove him to the tallest peaks of sudoku. No one can take it away from him. The best and most emotional part of representing Australia was singing the anthem and hearing that crowd belting out *'Advance Australia Fair'*. Can you imagine the tingle in the spine when Mick heard 100,000 cheering for him, or against him, with his pencil in hand in that arena? He has worn the green and gold and he played clean and hard like all Aussies. For mine, Colliss, Skiffington and the Sutherland brothers are legends.

Phil Kearns, former Wallaby captain
and Rugby World Cup gold medallist

Acknowledgements

William Webb Ellis is the man credited with founding the game of rugby. He was a student at the Rugby school in England in 1823 when he, in complete disregard for the rules of football as it was played at the time, picked up the ball and ran with it.

Sandy Sutherland is the William Webb Ellis of Australian sudoku. If he didn't 'pick up the ball and run with it' when I first suggested travelling to India to play sudoku for Australia, I would never have worn the green and gold and represented my country at the World Sudoku Championship. I am forever in his debt and remain eternally grateful for his positive response. I can't thank him enough.

Similar thanks are extended to my Australian team mates Skiffo and Hamish. It was an honour to compete alongside them at the highest level.

To Paul Kelly from Members Equity bank and David Sierakowski from Scout Entertainment, your generosity and assistance added another dimension to our trip. On behalf of the Members Equity Numbats Australian Sudoku Team, thank you.

Special thanks are extended to Radio 6PR's 'Breakfast Show' producer Ryan Rampling, who volunteered his services as the Numbat's media manager. Congratulations on a job well done. To co-host Steve Mills, Program Director John Solvander and General Manager Declan Kelly, thank you for your continued support.

To Scott Baskett and Michael Green, the Director and Producer of *Colours By Numbers, the Sudokumentary*, thank you for not only enjoying our story, but for deciding to tell it. I hope you're both well rewarded for your efforts.

If there was a Best on Ground award given out at the World Sudoku Championship, it would have gone to sudokumentary cameraman Bayden Findlay. 'Baydos' didn't stop working from the moment we left till the moment we returned. Mate, you are a champion. I look forward to the next time we can share a Kingfisher or three.

When I thought there might be a book in this adventure, the first person I called was Nigel Marsh. We met after I read his book *Fat, Forty and Fired* and I've classed him as a mate ever since. His enthusiasm for my project was infectious and his advice was invaluable. Nige, thanks for watering the seed.

As soft as it sounds, a love of poetry is what brought Rupert McCall and me together. He remains a mentor and a mate and I can't thank him enough for putting me in touch with some of the sports people who kindly provided quotes for this book. I still owe him a six pack from a failed wager on a recent State of Origin series. I look forward to sharing it with him.

If someone told me I'd one day be thanking Dennis Lillee, Phil Kearns, Rechelle Hawkes, Wally Lewis, Peter FitzSimons and John Eales in the acknowledgements section of a book I'd written, I'd tell them I had more chance of playing sudoku for Australia. These people have been idols of mine for a long time. It's humbling they agreed to contribute. I'd especially like to thank Fitz, not only for the endorsement on the cover, but for the help and advice he has been so generous in giving over the years. The same goes to John for writing the Foreword. He was a magnificent ambassador for rugby when he was playing, and remains one of the true gentlemen of Australian sport. I feel honoured to have his name associated with my story.

To my agent, Margaret Kennedy, I owe you one. Even if you are a Queensland Reds supporter. You saw something in this that others didn't. Without you, the manuscript would be nothing more than scrap for my kids to make paper planes out of.

The same thanks go to the wonderful people at ABC Books. It's been a real honour to have them in my corner. To my publisher Brigitta Doyle, publicist Jordan Weaver and editor Jo Butler, thank you for your time and effort. Everything you've done has been hugely appreciated.

When I'm not busy representing my country, I work at Cooch Creative, a regional advertising consultancy in Perth. To Ron Samuel, Espedito Mario Benito Battista, Alf Scalise and Aleisha Zappia, and to Josh Bolto from Trinet Media, thanks for not taking the piss out of me when I said I wanted to be an international sudoku player.

Thanks also to Anton De St Pern from Thrifty WA; Rania Challis from Coco's; Mark Gibson and Andrea Burns from Channel Seven; Russell Hearnden from EmbroidMe; Paul Ramsay from Travel & Sports Australia; Leith Putland from Lion Nathan; Helen Appleyard from

Moet-Hennessy; Meredith Eddington from UWA and Imagesource for supplying Cut-Out Sandy.

Like most people who are given the honour of wearing the green and gold, I carried the best wishes of many people with me on my journey. People who supported me at various stages of my life and shared my dream. In their own way, they've influenced me more than they know. To my mother, Mary, who was always happy to do a loaves and fishes to feed my hungry mates, and to my father, Wazza, for always being involved with my junior teams, first as a manager and then as a strapper. I know switching codes from league to union was like switching religions, but, I'm sure you'll agree, rugby's given us all more joy and stronger friendships than we could have imagined. To my co-best man Brian Maguire; paddling partner Bernard Walsh; Hawkesbury Classic crewman P. Rick Butler; Bledisloe Cup tourists Sarah Carne and Mark Ferdinand; Bledisloe Cup tour host Lee Carseldine; and my many former housemates, especially Marty Roebuck, Mark Skiffington, Stephen Boyle, Andrew Harris and Erin Kennedy, my sincere thanks.

I'd also like to thank you for taking the time to read our story. I hope you enjoyed it.

Last but by no means least, I'd like to thank my wife, Sharan. She's been the one consistent in my life. Which is not always a good thing.

When I was first picked in the Australian team, I thought I was a certainty to get some sweet loving. But I was wrong. When I returned home from the tournament, I thought she would be waiting to welcome me back in the nicest possible way. But no, she was away on a water polo trip.

When ABC Books offered me the contract — a huge moment for me — I tried to convince her that 'Celebratory Sex' was a legitimate event. She wasn't interested.

Maybe one day she'll surprise me.

Then again, maybe she won't. She was looking through a sports magazine a few weeks ago and saw an ad for premature ejaculation. She said to me, 'That sounds good. Why don't you buy some?'

Sharan was a huge support to me during the writing process and read each chapter as I finished it. If she laughed at something, I kept it in. If she thought something was daft, she'd tell me and invariably she'd be right. Sharan is everything an Australian representative should be. She loves her sport, has a training ethic unmatched by anyone I've ever met, and constantly amazes me how hard she can push herself. The fact she remains a key player at forty years of age in a side that has won four of the past five national tournaments is testament to both her ability and her character.

Most importantly, she's a fantastic mother to our boys, Matt and Ben, two gorgeous young kids who will one day be extremely proud to say both their parents vice-captained Australia at a world championship.